Eller / Vogel

Information Security and Prototype Protection According to ISA 6 & TISAX®

Christopher Eller
Bennet Vogel

Information Security and Prototype Protection According to ISA 6 & TISAX®

Understand and Implement Requirements Successfully

HANSER

TISAX® is a registered trademark of the ENX Association.
VDA® is a registered trademark of the German Association of the Automotive Industry.

Print-ISBN: 978-1-56990-496-1
E-Pub-ISBN: 978-1-56990-962-1
E-Book-ISBN: 978-1-56990-959-1

Bibliographic information of the German National Library:
The German National Library lists this publication in the German National Bibliography; detailed bibliographic data are available on the Internet at http://dnb.d-nb.de.

Vilshofener Straße 10 | 81679 Munich | info@hanser.de
www.hanserpublications.com
www.hanser-fachbuch.de
Editor: Lisa Hoffmann-Bäuml
Production Management: Eberl & Koesel Studio, Kempten
Cover concept: Marc Müller-Bremer, www.rebranding.de, Munich
Cover design: Max Kostopoulos
Cover picture: shutterstock.com/Gorodenkoff
Typesetting: le-tex publishing services GmbH, Leipzig

Content

Foreword to the English edition

With currently over 50,000 certified locations, TISAX ® has become the second largest standard for Information Security worldwide.

TISAX® is a label used to demonstrate the fulfilment of safety requirements set by large automotive companies and does not only apply to "typical suppliers" in the automotive sector. Virtually every company that supplies a European OEM (Original Equipment Manufacturer) or major supplier is already obliged to fulfil OEM requirements. This affects companies of all kinds: in addition to suppliers of automotive parts, also advertising agencies, management consultancies, photographers, software companies and many more.

The requirements of automotive manufacturers are published in a standard-like format as the "ISA catalogue" (ISA: Information Security Assessment), relate to information security and are therefore – apart from the special case of prototype protection – useful for almost every company. Companies with the TISAX® label generally achieve a level of information security comparable to ISO 27001 and in many cases even higher.

With the English edition of this book, we are responding to the growing demand from companies worldwide for a practical guide to implementing TISAX. Based on our second German edition, this book provides up to date information based on the latest version of the ISA Catalogue: We cover all Information Security and Prototype Protection requirements of this catalogue.

This book is based on the currently valid version 6.0.3 of the ISA catalogue, including the criteria catalogues "Information Security & Prototype Protection" (as of June 2025).

We have written the book in clear, practice-oriented language that is understandable without prior knowledge. Our aim is to enable the best possible understanding of the TISAX® requirements while providing directly implementable recommendations.

Darmstadt and Berlin, summer 2025

Christopher Eller

Bennet Vogel

Notes

This work addresses the "Information Security Assessment" standard in version 6.0.3:

- Publisher: © 2023 ENX Association, an Association under the French Law of 1901, registered under No. w923004198 at the Sous-préfecture of Boulogne-Billancourt, France.
- The "Data Protection" tab is provided, owned and copyrighted by VERBAND DER AUTOMOBILINDUSTRIE e. V. (VDA, German Association of the Automotive Industry); Behrenstr. 35; 10117 Berlin
- Source: *https://portal.enx.com/de-de/TISAX/downloads*
- This work is licensed under the Creative Commons Attribution-NoDerivatives 4.0 International Public License.

In the text of the book, chapter headings and the boxes labeled "Quotation from the VDA® ISA 6.0.3" cite this standard. The organizational structure of the book is based on the standard.

The authors of this book are not part of or affiliated with VDA® or ENX®. The following trademarks are mentioned:

- TISAX® is a registered trademark of the ENX® Association.
- VDA® is a registered trademark of the German Association of the Automotive Industry.
- ISO is a registered trademark of the International Organization for Standardization.
- DIN is a registered trademark of the German Institute for Standardization.

The VDA has updated the "Information Security Assessment" and made it available for download. Available at *https://portal.enx.com/de-de/TISAX/downloads*.

Foreword to the 2nd edition

The ISA catalogue in version 6 has been mandatory for new TISAX assessments since spring 2024.

The new version of the standard was first published primarily and initially in English and is now available directly on the ENX® website. The addition of "VDA®" of "VDA ISA" has already been largely dropped in the publications, and ENX® itself now only refers to the catalogue as "ISA" in many places. This is a clear sign that TISAX® will be used even more widely in the European automotive industry in the future.

It is now also possible to present the certification achieved, for example on the website or on a certificate in the entrance area, thanks to a "decorative document": *https://portal.enx.com/en-us/news/New-decorative-TISAX-assessment-document-now-available*

With the 2nd edition of this book, we are updating our recommendations for implementing the standard and expanding them to include the prototype protection module. We provide implementation recommendations for all new information security requirements from ISA 6. Organizations that handle physical prototypes in accordance with TISAX® requirements will now also find implementation recommendations for this that are compatible with the recommendations for information security.

Feedback on the 1st edition as well as typical questions that were brought to us in discussions with consulting clients and audits have also been incorporated into the 2nd edition. We are grateful for this valuable input, which has enabled us to make the book even more practice-orientated.

Interest in TISAX® continues to be high in Germany, even from companies that have had no previous contact with the topic, and we are also receiving an increasing number of international enquiries. With the 2nd edition of the book, we want to give even more companies easy access to TISAX®.

We have based this book on the currently valid version 6.0.2 of the ISA catalogue with the criteria catalogues "Information Security & Prototype Protection" (as of August 2024).

Darmstadt and Berlin, summer 2024

Christopher Eller

Bennet Vogel

Notes

This work deals with the "Information Security Assessment" standard in version 6.0.2:

- Publisher: © 2023 ENX Association, an Association according to the French Law of 1901, registered under No. w923004198 at the Sous-préfecture of Boulogne-Billancourt, France.
- The "Data Protection" tab is provided, owned and copyrighted by VERBAND DER AUTOMOBILINDUSTRIE e. V. (VDA, German Association of the Automotive Industry); Behrenstr. 35; 10117 Berlin
- Source: *https://portal.enx.com/de-de/TISAX/downloads*
- This work is licensed under the Creative Commons Attribution-NoDerivatives 4.0 International Public Licence.

In the text of the book, the chapter headings and the boxes "Quotation from the VDA® ISA 6.0.2" quote from this standard. The organizational structure of the book is based on the standard.

The authors of this book are not part of or affiliated with VDA® or ENX®. The following trademarks are mentioned:

- TISAX® is a registered trademark of the ENX® Association.
- VDA® is a registered trademark of the German Association of the Automotive Industry.
- ISO is a registered trademark of the International Organization for Standardization.
- DIN is a registered trademark of the German Institute for Standardization.

The VDA has updated the "Information Security Assessment" and made it available for download. Available at *https://portal.enx.com/de-de/TISAX/downloads*.

Preface to the 1st edition

TISAX® is a label used to demonstrate the fulfilment of security requirements of large German automotive companies and does not apply only to "typical suppliers" in the automotive sector.

The requirements of automotive manufacturers are published in a standard-like manner as the "VDA® ISA Catalogue" (VDA: German Association of the Automotive Industry; ISA: Information Security Assessment), relate to information security and are therefore – apart from the special case of prototype protection – useful for almost every company. Companies with the TISAX® label generally achieve a level of information security comparable to ISO 27001 and in many cases even higher.

Virtually every company that supplies an OEM (Original Equipment Manufacturer) or major supplier is already obliged to fulfil the requirements of OEMs or will be in the near future. This affects companies of all kinds: In addition to suppliers of automotive parts, this also includes advertising agencies, management consultancies, photographers, software houses and many more.

The content of the VDA® ISA catalogue is based on the ISO 27001 standard. Older editions of the VDA® ISA up to version number 4 therefore have a similar chapter structure. Version 5 of the VDA® ISA catalogue introduced a completely new chapter structure. The link to ISO 27001 is no longer recognizable at first glance. This "cutting of the cord" from ISO 27001 speaks for the increased self-confidence of ENX® and VDA® in having established a success story with TISAX®.

If you are already familiar with ISO standards and the usual audit procedures, much of the "TISAX® world" will also seem familiar to you. There is also a standard here, but in the form of an Excel spreadsheet in which you can directly enter information on the implementation of the standard requirements. There are also audits – referred to here as inspections – but only once every three years. Instead of a DAkkS, the ENX® has overall supervision of the authorized certification bodies – which are known as assessment service providers at TISAX®. You only have to do without the beloved certificate on the wall – the *TISAX®* labels can only be viewed electronically in the ENX® portal.

A few notes on the use of this book: When we refer to “the standard” or “TISAX® requirements”, we mean the requirements of the VDA® ISA catalogue, which are then assessed in the TISAX® procedure and the results of which are shared with other companies. The assessment to achieve the TISAX® label is comparable to a certification audit, which is why we refer to this assessment synonymously as an audit.

The chapters are written in the same order as in the VDA® ISA catalogue. We have also adopted the chapter titles and numbering one-to-one. This gives you, the reader, the greatest benefit, as you can use this book as a reference book to quickly gain clarity on individual TISAX® requirements.

We have written the book in clear language that is consistently practice-orientated and understandable without prior knowledge. Our aim is to enable the best possible understanding of the TISAX® requirements and at the same time to provide directly realizable recommendations for implementation.

The editorial deadline for this book was October 2022, based on the currently valid version 5.1.0 of the VDA® ISA catalogue and the Information Security test objective.

Darmstadt and Berlin, spring 2023

Christopher Eller

Bennet Vogel

Notes

This work deals with the standard “VDA® ISA” in version 5.1.0.

- Published by: VERBAND DER AUTOMOBILINDUSTRIE e. V. (VDA); Behrenstr. 35; 10117 Berlin; *www.vda.de* © 2022 Verband der Automobilindustrie e. V., Berlin.
- Source: *https://www.vda.de/dam/jcr:6ea8f56e-8497-4e65-866d-d4cf98ea6e59/VDA_ISA_5_1_DE.xlsx*
- This work is licensed under the Creative Commons Attribution – No Derivatives 4.0 International Public Licence.

In the text of the book, the chapter headings and the boxes “Quotation from the VDA® ISA 5.1.0” quote from this standard. The organizational structure of the book is based on the standard.

The authors of this book are not part of or affiliated with VDA® or ENX®. The following trademarks are mentioned:

- TISAX® is a registered trademark of the ENX® Association.
- VDA® is a registered trademark of the German Association of the Automotive Industry.

- ISO is a registered trademark of the International Organization for Standardization.
- DIN is a registered trademark of the German Institute for Standardization.

The VDA has updated the "Information Security Assessment" and made it available for download. Available at *https://portal.enx.com/de-de/TISAX/downloads*.

1 IS Policies and Organization

1.1 Information security policies

1.1.1 To what extent are information security policies available?

Quote from ISA 6.0.3

The organization needs at least one information security policy. This reflects the importance and significance of information security and is adapted to the organization. Additional policies may be appropriate depending on the size and structure of the organization.

Must

- The requirements for information security have been determined and documented:
  - The requirements are adapted to the organization's goals
  - A policy has been prepared and approved by the organization
- The policy includes objectives and the significance of information security within the organization.

Should

- The information security requirements based on the strategy of the organization, legislation and contracts are considered in the policy.
- The policy indicates consequences in case of non-conformance.
- Other relevant security policies are established.
- Periodic review and, if required, revision of the policies is established.
- The policies are made available to employees in a suitable form (e.g. intranet).
- Employees and external business partners are informed of any changes relevant to them.

This section deals with the creation of at least one policy for information security. The standard aims to ensure that guidelines and requirements for information security are provided in writing. At least one information *security* policy must be created.

Implementation of the mandatory requirements

A **mandatory requirement** must be fulfilled. The fulfilment of a mandatory requirement cannot be ruled out.

Determine and document requirements

You create at least one central policy for information security *(information security policy)*. Such a policy is usually around ten to 15 pages long. It describes the following in particular (selection):

- A description of why information security is important for your company and how you intend to establish a high level of information security.
- A description of how your organization intends to ensure the confidentiality, availability and integrity of information (strategic approach).
- You set measurable targets *(KPI – Key Performance Indicator)* for information security for a defined period (e. g. Hiring two new employees in IT, introducing two-factor authentication for system X, purchasing a new server, etc.). As these objectives change regularly, it is advisable to describe them in a separate document (KPI) and refer to them in the central policy.
- General rules of conduct for handling information and the hardware and software provided (e. g. Prohibition of local storage of private files, rules of conduct in the event of loss of a company notebook, etc.).

The policy must be saved in a suitable form. The PDF format or an entry on the intranet is suitable here. It is important that the policy can only be edited by authorized persons.

We recommend including a version history in every policy. The policy must be officially approved. Either directly by the management or by a person authorized within the company to approve it. A signature in the document is not required by the standard. In any case, the date of approval and the name of the person authorizing the approval must be recognizable.

It is a good idea to refer to other individual policies in the central policy. For example, you can briefly describe the topic of virus protection or assigning user authorizations in the central policy and refer to the detailed descriptions in the respective individual policies. Alternatively, you can describe everything in the central *information security policy*, but then you will quickly end up with 150 pages or more. This is unusual but permitted by the standard.

Policy is not the same as policy!

TISAX requires a policy similar to the requirements of ISO 27001, Control A.5.1. It does not (!) require a policy similar to the requirements of ISO 27001, clause 5.2. The latter is rather a description a mission statement, and usually up to one page long. If you already have such a document, you can of course keep it, but it will not be audited in your TISAX assessment.

Implementation of the should requirements

A **should requirement** should be fulfilled, but if there is a comprehensible reason for not fulfilling it, it can be excluded.

Extended requirements

You also describe the following in the central *guideline on information security*:

- A description from a management perspective of why information security is important to your organization, in particular the strategic importance and the importance with regard to applicable laws and contractual agreements.
- Responsibilities (e. g. Information Security Officer – ISO, Data Protection Officer, system administrators) are named, e. g. in a function matrix.
- You indicate the consequences under labor law and possible criminal law (it is not necessary to specify individual laws or paragraphs) in the event that employees violate the policy. Further requirements in Section 2.1.1.

Determine and document testing and other guidelines

Other guidelines – as described – must also be stored and released in a suitable form.

The guidelines must be accessible to all persons affected by them, preferably by filing them in a suitable folder structure. In the event of changes to the guidelines, the affected persons inside and outside the company must be informed. If necessary, individual contents can also be passed on to business partners. This point is playing an increasingly important role in practice, as companies are being asked more and more frequently to make individual policies available to their clients as part of self-assessments.

Check all guidelines regularly – at least once a year – to ensure that they are up to date and complete. It is best to schedule these check(s) in your centralized action list *(action plan)* or as a serial appointment in your calendar. The review carried out must always be documented, even if you do not make any changes to the content of the documents. Table 1.1 shows an example of how an action plan could be structured.

Table 1.1 Action plan (example)

ID	Requirement	Measure	Responsible	Date	Examination
...	...	...	...	...	...
...	...	...	...	...	...

1.2 Organization of information security

The standard requirement describes the requirements for organizational structures and measures for implementing information security. The requirement to set up an information security management system (ISMS) is derived centrally from this.

1.2.1 To what extent is information security managed within the organization?

Quote from ISA 6.0.3

Only if information security is part of the strategic goals of an organization, information security can be implemented in an organization in a sustainable manner. The information security management system (ISMS) is a control mechanism used by the organization's management to ensure that information security is the result of sustainable management rather than that of mere coincidence and individual effort.

Must

- The scope of the ISMS (the organization managed by the ISMS) is defined.
- The organization's requirements for the ISMS are determined.
- The organizational management has commissioned and approved the ISMS.
- The ISMS provides the organizational management with suitable monitoring and control means (e.g. management review).
- Applicable controls have been determined (e.g. ISO 27001 Statement of Applicability, completed ISA catalogue).
- The effectiveness of the ISMS is regularly reviewed by the management.

Basically, your organization needs to define the structure, responsibilities and means of information security compliance to ensure that "information security" is implemented within the intended framework and that the desired results are achieved.

Implementation of the mandatory requirements

Defining the scope

In order to explain which scope your company is aiming for the ISMS, a document (declaration of applicability or *scope*) should be created in which you explain:

- Which standard, including version number, does the company use to implement the ISMS?
- Which assessment level and which test objectives have been selected?
- Which locations does the ISMS cover (including the addresses)?
- What specific inclusions or exclusions apply?

The document should be approved by the management.

Structure for formulating the scope (example)

1. Applicable standard
2. Processes
3. Departments
4. Locations
5. Networks
6. Resources
7. Exclusions from the scope of application
8. Responsibilities

Restriction of the scope

In principle, it is possible to limit the scope of your ISMS.

For example, it is conceivable to apply the ISMS-specific regulations only to certain departments that are involved in order processing for OEMs. However, remember that interfaces to standard processes that can influence the ISMS (personnel, IT, physical security) remain in any case.

Limiting the scope within a location is therefore usually only sensible if there are very different areas of activity and the areas of activity without security requirements/OEM reference should be left out for reasons of cost.

It is therefore advisable to use the "standard scope".

Determining requirements and commissioning the ISMS

To determine and document the requirements of the ISMS organization, include an introductory section in your *information security policy* to document the basic security requirements (your company's requirements, customer requirements, positioning in relation to the competition) and your position and objectives in this regard.

The *information security policy* should be approved by the company management in order to make it clear that the top management commits behind the objectives.

Control means and monitoring

Control in the set of management tools involves the planning and implementation of measures to achieve a specific goal. **Effectiveness** is the extent to which the intended results are achieved. Audits are, for example, **effectiveness reviews**. They are used to check the effectiveness of the management system.

In order to regularly review the effectiveness of the ISMS, you should conduct a *management review* at least once a year in which the Information Security Officer and the management discuss the following topics:

- Current developments in ISMS
- Audits performed and planned
- Changes to the scope
- Developments at suppliers, customers and interested parties with regard to information security
- Changes in documents and guidelines
- Current risk situation
- Status of measures
- Training courses organized
- Key figures
- Security incidents

The *management review* should be recorded together with the content discussed and made available to all participants by the Information Security Officer.

The *management review* is also known as the *management assessment*.

Determining the controls

In principle, you must also determine all applicable controls (also known as controls, which refers to the standard chapters of the standard) of the standard ("Which chapters of the catalogue are applicable to me?"). To do this, document the maturity level and a description of implementation ("Which rules have you implemented in practice?") in the catalogue for each chapter after implementation.

In the past, exclusion was often possible in areas of mobile working or the use of cloud services if this was not applicable.

A requirement can be declared as **"not applicable"** if it does not play a role for a company, e. g. if there is no cloud usage.

In practice, however, hardly any exclusion is accepted, as companies have now largely made these cases the norm through the use of home offices and cloud services, or it is at least foreseeable that these and similar issues could play a role in the company.

If these issues still do not apply to you, it is therefore advisable to consider the chapters as applicable (i.e. you check your security regulation in accordance with the requirements of the standard) and set up prohibition rules in practice. In this way, you can prove that these aspects have nevertheless been taken into account.

1.2.2 To what extent are information security responsibilities organized?

Quote from ISA 6.0.3

A successful ISMS requires clear responsibilities within the organization.

Must

- Responsibilities for information security within the organization are defined, documented, and assigned.
- The responsible employees are defined and qualified for their task.
- The required resources are available.
- The contact persons are known within the organization and to relevant business partners.

Should

- There is a definition and documentation of an adequate information security structure within the organization.
- Other relevant security roles are considered.

Additional requirements high

- An appropriate organizational separation of responsibilities should be established in order to avoid conflict of interests (separation of duties).

In order to operate information security management successfully and effectively, it is necessary to clearly define responsibilities.

Implementation of the mandatory requirements

Document the responsibilities of all key positions involved in the ISMS for the requirement. This can be done in the *information security policy*, for example. Typical responsibilities may lie with the following roles:

- **Information Security Officer (ISO):** Development and maintenance of the ISMS, identification of risks, reporting to management, processing of information security incidents.
- **Management:** Providing the necessary resources, acting as a role model for information security, communicating important security-related topics to the workforce.
- **IT management/CIO:** Close cooperation with the ISO in analyzing risks and incidents as well as in developing the security strategy and measures
- **Data Protection Officer/DPO:** Work closely with the ISO to assess risks, coordinate the security strategy and develop measures to comply with legal requirements.
- **Management:** Acting as a role model, close cooperation with the ISO, support in assessing information security risks.
- **Staff:** Compliance with information security regulations, reporting of incidents.
- All roles that may be relevant to information security should be considered. Depending on the size of the company, this may also explicitly include quality management or the CFO, for example, as these positions can make important decisions with an impact on the ISMS.

The ISO should also be named. To do this, proceed as follows:

- Appoint the ISO in writing with a letter of appointment that sets out the tasks, resources (in terms of time and money) and requirements.
- Consider the ISO as a staff unit in the organization chart.
- The contact details of the ISO should be explicitly communicated to the staff once again (e. g. via email or as part of the information security training).
- Where applicable, the contact details can also be passed on to customers and suppliers, for example to enable incidents to be reported.

Qualification of the Information Security Officer (ISO)

Even if the standard does not explicitly specify the qualification of the person responsible for information security, it is advisable to ensure this and to take it into account in the appointment certificate.

Typical and possible qualifications are, for example, participation in an ISO training course with a recognized training service provider, previous experience in IT, quality management or as a data protection officer.

If your ISO does not have a strong technical background, close cooperation with IT can be anchored in the structure.

In addition, in order to fulfil the standard requirement for employee qualification, it should be possible to demonstrate that employees are generally qualified for their work through job advertisements and recruitment procedures.

Implementation of the should requirements

You fulfil the requirement by setting up an *information security policy*, assigning responsibilities and establishing guidelines, management and control instruments (risk management, audits, *management review*) to create a functional ISMS. You can also create a system landscape to illustrate the key instruments and interactions of your ISMS. This is shown as an example in Figure 1.1.

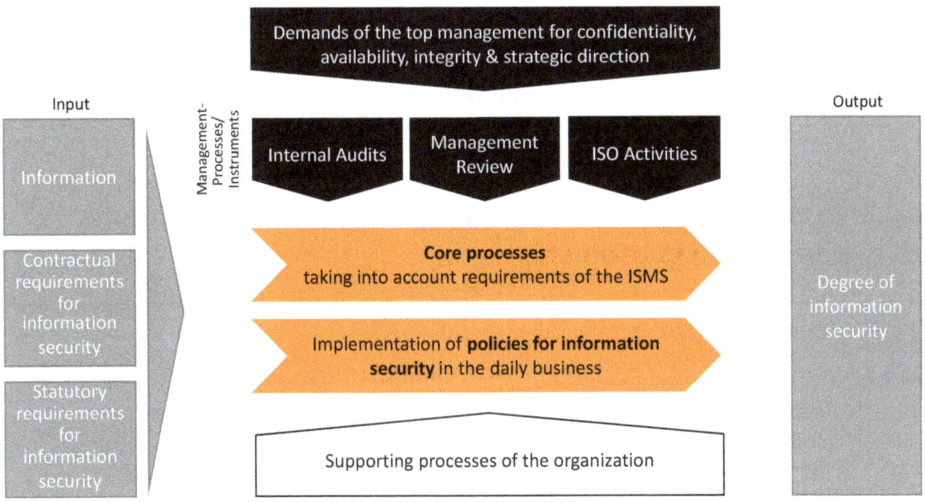

Figure 1.1 Example ISMS system landscape (illustration from BV, 2025)

Implementation of the additional requirements for "high" protection requirements

In principle, functions that are in conflict of interest should be separated.

In the context of information security, this includes, for example, the fact that the ISO may have other interests than the management. For this reason, roles should be separated where possible and the ISO should not be a member of management, for example.

However, the standard explicitly refers to an appropriate separation. If a separation is not possible for you (e.g. because your company is small or the best qualified person for information security is a member of the management), these conflicts should be explicitly documented together with countermeasures. A risk assessment should also be carried out and documented in the risk matrix.

Conflict of interest (example)

Information Security Officer (ISO) and management: If the ISO is also a member of the management, there is a fundamental conflict. The ISO, for example, has high expectations in terms of information security and would like to receive the corresponding budget for this. The management has an interest in minimizing the complexity of processes and saving resources.

In this situation, it would be conceivable to implement various measures to minimize the conflict of interest and, for example, to conduct the *management review* together with the shareholders. Ideally, this constellation should be avoided.

ISO and IT management: If the ISO is also in charge of IT, independent monitoring of IT activities (e.g. checking event logs, analyzing security incidents) cannot be guaranteed.

If this constellation cannot be avoided, it would be conceivable to use an external service provider to carry out control tasks (internal audits, review of event logs). Ideally, however, there should also be a separation of personnel here.

1.2.3 To what extent are information security requirements considered in projects?

Quote from ISA 6.0.3

For project implementation, it is important to consider the information security requirements. This applies to projects within the organization regardless of their type. By appropriately establishing the information security process in the project management procedures of the organization, any overlooking of requirements is prevented.

Must

- Projects are classified while taking into account the information security requirements.

Should

- The procedure and criteria for the classification of projects are documented.
- During an early stage of the project, risk assessment is conducted based on the defined procedure and repeated in case of changes to the project.
- For identified information security risks, measures are derived and considered in the project.

Additional requirements high

- The measures thus derived are reviewed regularly during the project and reassessed in case of changes to the assessment criteria.

To fulfil the requirement, proceed as follows:

All projects in the company should be classified according to their information security requirements. To this end, the ISO should be involved in the planning phase of projects.

Decisive criteria for this can be

- the classification of the information processed in the project (confidential, strictly confidential)
- the influence of the project on the future security level (structural measures, change of supplier or IT migrations)
- Financial risks due to non-compliance with security requirements or security incidents (contractual claims from customers)

Projects can then be categorized according to the levels internal, confidential and strictly confidential. The classification should be documented, e. g. in an ISO project overview or, better still, directly in the project management system so that all project participants are informed.

Customer projects must also be taken into account! If the activity for a customer remains the same, the framework agreement with the customer (OEM) can be considered a project.

Implementation of the should requirements

Create documentation (project management guideline) that describes the criteria you use to classify projects and how you document this classification.

The documentation should contain a simple flowchart or RACI matrix for projects to record the necessary steps in the planning, implementation and acceptance of projects from the perspective of the ISMS. This should include

- Involving the ISO in an early phase of the project to carry out the classification.
- In the case of confidential and strictly confidential projects, the ISO should carry out a risk assessment together with the project manager and derive any necessary measures.
- The risk assessment should be repeated if changes are made to the project.

A RACI matrix is a frequently used visualization of work steps and the associated distribution of tasks. A sequence of work steps is listed one below the other in a matrix. On the right are columns for the four categories

- R = Responsible: responsible for the implementation,
- A = Accountable: accountable in the sense of commercial or legal responsibility,
- C = Consulted: to be consulted in an advisory capacity,
- I = Informed: to inform.

Depending on the responsibility, these four columns contain names or abbreviations or even function designations. Columns C or I can remain empty for individual work steps. R and A must always be completed.

Implementation of additional requirements for "high" protection requirements

Expand the described flow chart:

- The measures should be monitored by the ISO during the project.
- At the end of the project, the measures should also be accepted/checked for implementation.

1.2.4 To what extent are the responsibilities between external IT service providers and the own organization defined?

Quote from ISA 6.0.3

It is important, that a common understanding of the division of responsibilities exists and that the implementation of all security requirements is ensured. Therefore, when using external IT service providers and IT services, the responsibilities regarding the implementation of information security measures are to be defined and verifiably documented.

Must

- The concerned services and IT services used are identified.
- The security requirements relevant to the IT service are determined:
- The organization responsible for implementing the requirement is defined and aware of its responsibility.
- Mechanisms for shared responsibilities are specified and implemented.
- The responsible organization fulfils its respective responsibilities.

Should

- In case of IT services, configuration has been conceived, implemented, and documented based on the necessary security requirements.
- The responsible staff is adequately trained.

Additional requirements high

- A list exists indicating the concerned IT services and the respective responsible IT service providers.
- The applicability of the ISA controls has been verified and documented.
- The service configuration is included in the regular security assessments.
- Proof is provided that the IT service providers fulfil their responsibility.
- Integration into local protective measures (such as secure authentication mechanisms) is established and documented.

As cloud services can be complex IT systems with extended configuration options and extensive contractual conditions, the standard aims to ensure the level of information security when using these services.

Implementation of the mandatory requirements

All cloud services used must be documented. It is advisable to create a table of the cloud services used in which the service name, service provider and the purposes for which the cloud service is used are documented. It should be noted that free cloud services should also be taken into account.

Separate and joint responsibilities

The use of cloud services represents an outsourcing of central tasks for the respective service: For example, the provider takes care of availability, network security and data backups.

The standard therefore aims to ensure that your organization identifies which information security services are provided by the provider.

If certain features are not provided or do not meet your security requirements, these circumstances must be identified.

The following examples are intended to illustrate this:

- **Responsibility with the cloud provider:** For internal systems, they require that critical patches are rolled out in good time with the help of patch management. The provider also contractually guarantees this. The responsibility therefore lies with the provider. The contractual assurance allows you to clearly specify and prove responsibility.
- **Your responsibility:** You require an internal data backup frequency of at least 24 hours. However, the provider does not carry out any data backups. You therefore back up the data from the cloud service yourself. The responsibility lies with your organization.
- **Responsibility shared:** The provider provides a web application firewall with typical security functions that protects the services used. However, the customer can configure the firewall. The responsibility for securing the services is therefore shared between the two parties. You can also exert considerable influence on the level of security.

Reference all chapters of the standard in this documentation. You should now specify for each chapter:

- Is this chapter relevant for the respective service (security requirement applicable)? Yes/no + Brief explanation.
- Which organization (you or the cloud provider) is responsible for implementation? Or: Is the responsibility shared? Yes/no + Brief description of the situation.
- A reference to the proof of fulfilment of the responsibility (e. g. for provider contract chapters, reference to information security supplementary agreement, AV contract, written commitments from providers).

Implementation of the should requirements

Create a checklist together with the specialist staff for each cloud service used, which takes into account all the necessary security requirements in the configuration of the services. This will ensure that the configuration of the services meets your requirements.

You should check the checklist regularly (e. g. annually) or if there are significant changes to the service (e. g. new functionality) to ensure that the configuration of the service meets your requirements.

The security configuration of cloud services can be complex. Make sure that your specialist staff are appropriately qualified/trained.

Security requirement checklist for cloud services (example)

- Are the GDPR guidelines taken into account?
- Can all data be completely deleted from the cloud service at any time?
- Are all rights in the cloud clearly regulated?
- Is the data in the cloud encrypted?
- Is a secure firewall used?
- Are regular backups carried out?
- Is authentication clearly and securely regulated?
- Is the server protected against damage?
- etc.

Implementation of additional requirements for "high" protection requirements

The fulfilment of the requirements "List of services", "Applicability of controls", "Service configuration check", "Proof of responsibility" is already ensured by the implementation of the "must" and "should" tasks as described above.

Check that cloud services are integrated into local security measures where possible. For example, it is also possible to connect cloud services to your single sign-on or only allow access to cloud resources for users from the local organizational network.

1.3 Asset management

This section deals with the company's assets (Assets). Assets are tangible or intangible things that are worth protecting. This section is specifically concerned with all assets that can play a role in information security.

1.3.1 To what extent are information assets identified and recorded?

Quote from ISA 6.0.3

It is important for each organization to know the information constituting its essential assets (e.g. business secrets, critical business processes, know-how, patents).

They are referred to as information assets. An inventory ensures that the organization obtains an overview of its information assets. Moreover, it is important to know the supporting assets (e.g. IT systems, services/IT services, employees) processing these information assets.

Must

- Information assets and other assets where security is relevant to the organization are identified and recorded.
  - A person responsible for these information assets is assigned
- The supporting assets processing the information assets are identified and recorded:
  - A person responsible for these supporting assets is assigned

Should

- A catalogue of the relevant information assets exists:
  - The corresponding supporting assets are assigned to each relevant information asset
  - The catalogue is subject to regular review

Implementation of the mandatory requirements

Documenting assets

You create an inventory of assets of the company. This is best done in the form of a table.

Assets can be e.g.:

- Types of information from customers that are entrusted to you, e.g. Design drawings, construction plans, information about planned products or strategies
- Information from your own company, e.g. Source codes, patents, confidential process descriptions

- Software that you use in your company
- Types of data carriers that you use in your company
- Business processes

For better clarification, Table 1.2 shows a small excerpt from an exemplary asset inventory.

Table 1.2 Extract from an asset inventory (example)

Asset type	Designation	Asset manager	Information carrier of the asset
Information	CAD data from our customers	Operations management	Own server/Microsoft 365/CAD software XY
Software	ERP software XY	IT management	Own server
Free web service	DeepL	IT management	Cloud/Web
Hardware	Windows notebooks	IT management	Windows notebooks

Companies usually determine a two to three-digit number of assets. Please also note: The asset inventory is primarily about identifying categories of assets, not about listing every single asset. If you have been entrusted with around 40 infrastructure plans by customers, it is sufficient to enter infrastructure plans as a single entry in the "Customer information"-category in the inventory. The infrastructure plans are already stored in detail elsewhere and do not need to be listed individually here.

You assign a person responsible to each of these assets and describe the information carrier on which the asset is processed.

You will quickly notice that there are overlaps. These overlaps are even helpful in giving you a comprehensive picture of your assets.

The overlaps are because information is almost always processed with software and stored on data carriers. However, you not only consider the respective information as an asset, but also the software and the data carrier individually as an asset.

Implementation of the should requirements

Information carrier

You add a column to the asset inventory in which you indicate whether the asset is critical or not. You are free to decide which criteria you use to determine criticality. Assets are usually categorized as critical if their disclosure (loss of confidentiality) or loss (loss of integrity or availability) could lead to significant financial or business damage or threaten significant legal consequences.

You review the asset inventory at least once a year and adjust it if necessary. You plan the inspection as an action, for example in a central *action plan* or as a serial appointment in your calendar. Every check carried out and every update must be documented. Archive old versions of the asset inventory.

A common misunderstanding!

When it comes to asset management, companies often only think of an inventory of issued hardware. Time and again, you see asset inventories that list every single notebook issued and the number of monitors and printers in the company in detail, but do not contain any details about information worthy of protection.

This is completely inadequate in terms of an ISMS and is very likely to lead to deviations in the audit.

For example, your hardware and software should be inventoried in a configuration management database (CMDB). However, the documentation of this hardware and software is not the focus of Section 1.3.

It's not just about electronic documents!

Also note the assets that are not stored electronically. You may have design drawings on microfilm or personnel files in paper form. These are also assets.

That's why the asset inventory is so important!

The asset inventory forms the foundation for the introduction of your ISMS. This is about the security of information. You can only systematically increase the security of information if you are aware of the information that is worth protecting.

The correct categorization of risks that affect these assets is also only possible if you know the protection requirements of your assets.

By creating an asset inventory, you gain clarity about the existing assets and therefore the information that needs to be protected.

1.3.2 To what extent are information assets classified and managed in terms of their protection needs?

Quote from ISA 6.0.3

The objective of classifying information assets is the consistent determination of their protection needs. For this purpose, the asset the information has for the organization is determined based on the protection goals of information security (confidentiality, integrity, and availability) and classified according to a classification scheme. This enables the organization to implement adequate protective measures.

Must

- A consistent scheme for the classification of information assets regarding the protection goal of confidentiality is available.

- Evaluation of the identified information assets is carried out according to the defined criteria and assigned to the existing classification scheme.
- Specifications for the handling of supporting assets (e. g. identification, correct handling, transport, storage, return, deletion/disposal) depending on the classification of information assets are in place and implemented.

Should

- The protection goals of integrity and availability are taken into consideration.

This section deals with the handling of information assets, in particular their labelling and the regulation of access rights.

Implementation of the mandatory requirements

Definition of a standardized classification scheme

You define a multi-level scheme for confidentiality levels. For example, the four levels:

- Public
- Internal
- Confidential
- Strictly confidential

A recommendation for defining the four levels can be found in detail at the following link: *https://www.vda.de/en/news/publications/publication/harmonization-of-classification-levels.*

You compare your previously created inventory of assets with your confidentiality scheme and determine which information assets should be assigned to which confidentiality level. For example: CAD drawings from customers are always "confidential".

Guidelines for handling

You record the scheme and the assignment in the form of a guideline, for example as a *guideline for information classification*. Here you also specify which regulations apply for storage, storage, transport and destruction for the respective confidentiality level in connection with the respective storage medium (e. g. electronic, paper form).

Example: All personnel files in paper form are confidential. They may only be stored in a locked cabinet. Only employees of the HR department, authorized signatories and the management have keys. A document shredder of at least security level P4 must be used for destruction.

Or: All CAD data provided by the OEM is confidential. They may not be sent as email attachments, but only via an encrypted file exchange platform. If the data is to be deleted, the IT department must be consulted to ensure that it is securely overwritten.

Apply all the points described in your company no later than the release of the guideline so that you can present the relevant evidence in the external audit.

Simplifications are possible

With electronic documents in particular, it can be time-consuming to label each individual document according to its confidentiality level. You should therefore use simplifications and standard classifications. For example, you can specify that all documents that are not explicitly labelled are always classified as "internal". You can also classify entire areas in MS Teams or in JIRA that are reserved for individual projects. For example, by specifying that project-related areas in JIRA or in MS Teams and all their content are always "confidential". Unauthorized access is prevented by the access authorizations to the respective areas.

Implementation of the should requirements

According to ISO 27000, integrity is the "property of accuracy and completeness".

You also check whether, in addition to confidentiality, the integrity and/or availability of information is sufficiently guaranteed when applying your policy. If necessary, adapt your policy. In any case, note in the policy that you have checked the protection objectives of integrity and availability.

Why is this important?

If you take measures to maximize the confidentiality of information, this can be at the expense of integrity or availability. It is conceivable that you may neglect data backup because you want to keep as few copies of files as possible for security reasons.

Or it is conceivable that access to documents is made so difficult by high protection measures that there are significant delays in the workflow. Availability is restricted.

The should requirements in this section serve to take all three protection goals into account appropriately.

1.3.3 To what extent is it ensured that only evaluated and approved external IT services are used for processing the organization's information assets?

Quote from ISA 6.0.3

Particularly in the case of external IT services that can be used at relatively low cost or free of charge, there is an increased risk that procurement and commissioning will be carried out without appropriate consideration of the information security requirements and that security therefore is not ensured.

Must

- External IT services are not used without explicit assessment and implementation of the information security requirements:
  - A risk assessment of the external IT services is available
  - Legal, regulatory, and contractual requirements are considered
- The external IT services have been harmonized with the protection need of the processed information assets.

Should

- Requirements regarding the procurement, commissioning and release associated with the use of external IT services are determined and fulfilled.
- A procedure for release in consideration of the protection need is established.
- External IT services and their approval are documented.
- It is verified at regular intervals that only approved external IT services are used.

This section deals with a sub-topic of asset management: The processing of assets in low-cost or free IT services. This includes, for example, Cloud services that are operated via a website.

Examples of such services are:

- File transfer services for sending even large files
- Image processing services, also for exotic file formats
- Online translation services
- File conversion services

These services are often free, and you don't even need a user account to use them.

The security risks are obvious: If you transfer or open confidential files or have confidential texts translated online, you do not know whether these files are stored by the service provider and who can access them.

Implementation of the mandatory requirements

You define which IT services are authorized. You specify that only authorized IT services may be used in your company.

To do this, first take stock. Find out which IT services are currently being used. To do this, you can look at analyses of websites visited or ask your employees. Please note: This is about the IT services used by the entire company, not just those of your IT department.

The next step is to check for each of these IT services what types of files/content (and therefore what types of assets!) are usually used. For example, if full contracts (including names and prices) are translated using Google Translate, this may pose an unacceptable risk. You yourself assess which provider is acceptable for you, taking into account the need for protection of the respective assets. You also check whether there are any legal or contractual requirements that stand in the way of using a particular IT service.

This review is also a risk assessment of the IT services and must be documented. The risk matrix of the ISMS (see Section 1.4) can be used for this purpose.

Implementation of the should requirements

You document the authorized IT services – e. g. in the central *information security policy*. Here you also document whether these IT services may be used for all types of assets or only for certain types of assets. The clearest presentation is in tabular form. Table 1.3 shows an example.

Table 1.3 Documentation of the released IT services (example)

Free web service: *https://www.deepl.com/translator*				
Authorized use:	Translations from/to other languages			
Confidentiality level of the processed content:	Public	internal	Confidential	strictly confidential
Applicable regulations:	No restrictions	No restrictions	Confidential content (e. g. Personal data, business figures, business secrets) may not be entered.	Use not permitted!

At the same time, point out to your employees that IT services that are not (!) on this list may not be used.

They also describe how and by whom further IT services are released. The process for this can be, for example: Any user can informally request the use of an additional IT service from the Information Security Officer. The officer carries out a risk assessment and documents it. The IT service is added to the *information security policy* and is hereby approved.

Finally, check at regular intervals (at least annually) whether "prohibited" IT services are being used. This can be checked as part of technical system audits or through audit interviews with users. The specifications from Section 1.5 must be observed for this type of audit!

Additional risks due to BYOD (bring your own device)

Not explicitly mentioned in the ISA catalogue, the approval of BYOD results in additional risks from IT services outside the organization.

Whenever a company allows or even encourages BYOD, sensitive information can end up on employees' privately used free web services. Here is a scenario to illustrate this:

An employee uses a free messenger or a free dating app on their private smartphone. The names, job titles and contact details of business partners are also stored on this smartphone. In addition, the employee regularly takes photos of prototype vehicles and prototype parts on his private smartphone on behalf of the company. The messenger and dating apps installed on his private smartphone have the technical authorization to read the phone book and the smartphone's image memory. The personal data and photos of prototypes may end up on the servers of the app operators, e.g. in China.

The authorization of BYOD should therefore be examined very carefully. If in doubt, BYOD should be avoided in the interests of information security.

1.3.4 To what extent is it ensured that only evaluated and approved software is used for processing the organization's information assets?

Quote from ISA 6.0.3

Information processing is mostly done using of specific software. Security issues in software will easily become a risk for the information processed. Accordingly, software must be appropriately managed.

Must

- Software is approved before installation or use. The following aspects are considered:
  - Limited approval for specific use-cases or roles
  - Conformance to the information security requirements
  - Software use rights and licensing
  - Source/reputation of the software
- Software approval also applies to special purpose software such as maint

Should

- The types of software such as firmware, operating systems, applications, libraries, device drivers to be managed are determined.
- Repositories of managed software exist
- The software repositories are protected against unauthorized manipulation
- Approval of software is regularly reviewed
- Software versions and patch levels are known

Additional requirements very high

- Additional requirements for software use (e.g., need for control or monitoring of usage) are determined (if any)

The use of software can entail risks, which is why software should be checked before use to ensure that it meets the necessary criteria in terms of security, quality, origin and license rights.

Implementation of the mandatory requirements

Software that is to be used in the company should undergo a formal approval process. Ideally, the associated information and decisions should also be centralized in order to prevent the formation of shadow IT or parallel structures. In practice, for small and medium-sized companies this often means that IT or ISO decide or are informed about the use of the software.

In the simplest case, you integrate the criteria for the procurement and release of software in the *IT procurement guideline* described in Section 5.3.1. This should include, in coordination with your security requirements and the expectations of the OEM:

- Requirements for the reputation and source of the software in relation to the security requirements
- Requirements for security aspects such as cryptography, integration into existing security measures such as SSO, compatibility with existing programs
- Acceptable license terms
- Procured software should generally also, if compatible with your organizational structure, be installed by a central office (IT) to ensure that the intended use (e.g. certain groups of people, certain data that is processed with it) is guaranteed.

Implementation of the should requirements

You should ensure that the software used is distributed and managed from centralized and secure sources. As a rule, this means that you install the software e.g. via GPO from a central directory, via MDM (AppStore) or a management software.

The solution used to distribute the software (e. g. AD, MDM) should make it possible to determine the status of the clients and the software in order to make any decisions (e. g. rolling out updates). This should already be possible with standard market solutions without further configuration.

Implementation of the additional requirements for "high" protection requirements

Special requirements that can further secure the use of the software (e. g. activation of log functions, deeper integration into operating system security settings) should be checked before use.

1.4 Risk management for information security

1.4.1 To what extent are information security risks managed?

Quote from ISA 6.0.3

Information security risk management aims at the timely detection, assessment and addressing of risks in order to achieve the protection goals of information security. It thus enables the organization to establish adequate measures for protecting its information assets under consideration of the associated prospects and risks. It is recommended to keep the information security risk management of an organization as simple as possible such as to enable its effective and efficient operation.

Must

- Risk assessments are carried out both at regular intervals and in response to events.
- Information security risks are appropriately assessed (e.g. for probability of occurrence and potential damage).
- Information security risks are documented.
- A responsible person (risk owner) is assigned to each information security risk. This person is responsible for the assessment and handling of the information security risks.

Should

- A procedure is in place defining how to identify, assess and address security risks within the organization.
- Criteria for the assessment and handling of security risks exist.
- Measures for handling security risks and the persons responsible for these are specified and documented:
  - A plan of measures or an overview of their state of implementation is followed
- In case of changes to the environment (e.g. organizational structure, location, changes to regulations), reassessment is carried out in a timely manner.

The identification and assessment of risks is a central component of a risk-driven ISMS. A procedure for assessing risks must be defined for this purpose. Risk assessments must be carried out regularly and measures must be derived from them.

Implementation of the must and should requirements

Formal procedure

Create a formal document *Risk Management Procedure* which describes:

- Who assesses risks: As a rule, this should be carried out by the ISO together with specialized departments.
- How often these assessments are carried out: at least annually and on an ad hoc basis in the event of changes.
- The data basis used for the assessment: This includes empirical assets from the experts involved, statistical data e. g. from monitoring systems or other sources such as infrastructure operators, specialist publications.

The implementation and updating of the risk assessment should be planned via the *action plan* and carried out at least once a year and whenever there are changes in the organization.

Risks affect company assets and therefore generally relate to the asset register. The asset owners should be involved in the identification and assessment in a joint dialogue. For an initial identification of risks, a survey of the asset owners and specialized personnel by the ISO is recommended.

Evaluation scheme

Information security risks should be assessed according to a defined scheme in terms of *the extent of damage* and *probability of occurrence.*

A three-by-three scheme is sufficient to start with. As you gain more experience in risk management and further differentiation is necessary, a four-by-four or five-by-five scheme can also be established.

Document the defined scheme in the *risk management procedure.* The classes shown in Table 1.4 are useful to start with.

The defined scheme and procedure are universal and can therefore also be applied to other chapters in which risk assessment plays a role (see Section 1.3.3, Section 1.6.3, Section 4.1.2 and Section 5.2.2).

The monetary amounts listed under "Amount of loss" should be adjusted according to the size of the company and its turnover.

The two defined categorization assets can be multiplied together to determine a *risk class.* You should determine which risk class is still acceptable for you. This is how you define the *acceptance threshold,* a prioritization of all risks.

Table 1.4 Classification of probability and loss amount (example)

Categorization of the probability		
1	Low probability	The risk is likely to occur every five years or less.
2	Medium probability	The risk is likely to occur every one to five years.
3	High probability	The risk is likely to occur every year or more frequently.
Categorization of the amount of damage		
1	Low damage on occurrence	Only minor financial losses (less than € 5000) and no damage to the company's image are incurred if the risk occurs. Contracts or legal obligations are not affected.
2	Average damage on occurrence	If the risk occurs, there is a significant financial loss (up to € 100,000) and the image can be damaged. Contracts or legal obligations are easily breached.
3	High damage on occurrence	If the risk occurs, the company's existence is threatened (over € 100,000) and/or its image is severely damaged. Contracts or legal obligations are breached significantly and in an unjustifiable manner.

The defined risk classes and their acceptance should be documented in the *risk management procedure.* An overview as shown in Table 1.5 is useful to start with.

Table 1.5 Documentation of the risk classes

Risk class	Result	Consequence
1	1 to 3 (e.g. 1 × 3)	The risk is accepted, and no further action is required.
2	4 (e.g. 2 × 2)	The risk exceeds the acceptance threshold, and further measures must be initiated.
3	6 to 9 (e.g. 2 × 3)/damage level 3	The risk exceeds the acceptance threshold, and the risk must be reduced to class 2 through measures. Regardless of the multiplication result, all risks with damage class 3 are categorized in risk class 3, as particularly high damage is not acceptable even if it occurs infrequently.

Carrying out the evaluation

Create a *risk assessment* table in which assessed risks are documented. The table should contain the following columns:

- Unique number of the risk
- Owner (person responsible for the risk and treatment)

- Data sources used for the assessment
- Detailed description of the risk
- Assessment of the damage class
- Assessment of the probability of occurrence
- Resulting risk class
- Description of whether the risk is accepted or treated
- Associated action numbers from the *action plan*
- Date on which the risk was last updated

The assessment of risks should be planned and coordinated by the ISO. Risks relevant to the company should be identified, described and evaluated with the involvement of relevant departments (e. g. IT, Facility Management, Sales).

For risks that exceed the acceptance threshold, explicit measures should be described and scheduled in the *action plan*. Once these (counter) measures have been finalized, the assessment should be updated.

"Power failure" risk assessment (example)

- Risk number: 1
- Owner: IT management
- Data sources: Empirical assets, statistics of local network operators
- Description: In the past, there were frequent power failures in the industrial area of the Musterstadt site (between eight and 20 minutes). Due to a faulty design of the UPS, network components such as routers and switches were not taken into account. In the event of a power outage at, there is no loss of data, but it is no longer possible to supply the WLAN infrastructure and provide an Internet connection. In this case, employees are unable to continue working despite having laptops with battery power. It is not possible to set up VPN connections through other locations, therefore no access to merchandise management, etc.
- Assessment of the damage class: 2
- Assessment of the probability of occurrence: 2
- Resulting risk class: 2
- Acceptance: Although the risk is within the acceptance criteria, the management would like to explicitly take further measures here.
- Measures in the action plan: 17 (expansion of the UPS for network components, deadline: 31 December)
- Updated: 30.03.

1.5 Assessment

This section deals with internal and external audits for the ISMS. The standard requires regular internal and external audits of the ISMS and also uses the alternative terms *assessment* and *review* in some controls.

1.5.1 To what extent is compliance with information security ensured in procedures and processes?

Quote from ISA 6.0.3

It is not sufficient to define information security requirements and to prepare and publish policies. It is important to regularly review their effectiveness.

Must

- Observation of policies is verified throughout the organization.
- Information security policies and procedures are reviewed at regular intervals.
- Measures for correcting potential non-conformities (deviations) are initiated and pursued.
- Compliance with information security requirements (e.g. technical specifications) is verified at regular intervals.
- The results of the conducted reviews are recorded and retained.

Should

- A plan for content and framework conditions (time schedule, scope, controls) of the reviews to be conducted is provided.

Implementation of the mandatory requirements

You carry out internal audits on a regular basis, i.e. at least once a year. You can commission an external person to do this (e.g. a management consultancy) or the audit can be carried out by one or more of your company's employees.

The internal auditor should always be independent of the audited topics. This means, for example: The person responsible for collecting and processing information security incidents in the company should not audit this activity themselves. Exceptions are possible in companies with only a few employees.

Audit results must always be documented. The best way to do this is in an audit report, which is protected against changes (a PDF is usually better than a Word file). The report must contain the following information, among others:

- Date of the audit
- Name of the auditor(s)

- Audited persons
- Audited processes and guidelines
- The standard (specification of the catalogue in the current version number, together with the assessment objectives and the assessment levels)
- Results of the audit
- Deviations (also known as *non-conformities*) must be clearly labelled as such

Contents of an audit plan/audit report (example)

- Period of Audit
- Type of audit
- Audit location
- Audit target
- Audit criteria
- Audit scope
- Audit method
- Auditor
- Audit participants
- Language
- Audit budget
- Auditee (the audited organization, e.g. an entire company or an individual department)
- Resources
- Results of previous audits

Deviations must be dealt with systematically. If you already have an ISO management system, you can use the corrective action process defined there as a guide (for requirements, see clause 10.2 of the ISO standards for management systems). In principle, a root cause analysis must be carried out for each deviation and the result documented. It must also always be checked which measures are required to correct the deviation (i.e. the recognized error) and prevent a recurrence of this or a similar deviation. All measures taken as a result must be documented and an effectiveness review (colloquially: performance review) must be carried out. All of this must be documented. You are free to decide how you document this. Many companies document this in a centralized *action plan*. The use of special forms (deviation report or corrective action plan) is also common.

Implementation of the should requirements

You create an *audit program* in which you document a rough preliminary planning of the audits for the next twelve months. Better for the next 36 months.

All planned audits must be entered here. As this is a rough plan, it is sufficient to enter them on a monthly or quarterly basis. Details on the individual audits are entered later in the respective *audit plan* of the audit. In the audit program, you plan both the audits of the ISMS and the audits of the technical IT systems (see Section 5.2.6).

You may already be familiar with an audit program from ISO management systems. If you already have an audit program, you can easily add the audits required for the standard to it.

Contents of an audit program (example)

- Period of the audit program, e.g.: 2026 to 2028
- Types of the respective audits, e.g.: internal audit
- Scheduled times of the audits, monthly or quarterly
- Locations of the company to be audited
- Planned duration of the audits, e.g.: 2 days
- Standard basis of the audit, e.g.: TISAX® or ISO 27001
- Planned audit team for the respective audit

Watch out for these traps!

Incorrectly used terms can lead to confusion and errors. This can be seen time and again when it comes to audits.

Section 5.2.6 of the standard uses the term system audit. This refers to audits of technical IT systems. However, the term system audit is used in the ISO world for audits of the management system itself. If you already have an ISMS in accordance with ISO 27001, your audit program may already contain the term system audit, but this most likely refers to the audit of the requirements of clauses 4 to 10 of ISO 27001.

There is often confusion about the audit program, as the terms audit framework, audit plan, annual audit plan, etc. are also frequently used for this. The standard does not prescribe any terms here, so you can choose freely. However, it makes sense to actually call the audit program by this name, as every auditor is familiar with it. The agenda for an individual audit should ideally be called an audit plan. This is the easiest way to avoid misunderstandings.

1.5.2 To what extent is the ISMS reviewed by an independent authority?

Quote from ISA 6.0.3

As an essential control mechanism, assessing the effectiveness of the ISMS from merely an internal point of view is insufficient. Additionally, an independent and therefore objective assessment shall be obtained at regular intervals and in case of fundamental changes.

Must

- Information security reviews are carried out by an independent and competent body at regular intervals and in case of fundamental changes.
- Measures for correcting potential deviations are initiated and pursued.

Should

- The results of conducted reviews are documented and reported to the management of the organization.

Implementation of the mandatory requirements

You have your ISMS reviewed (audited) by an external audit service provider every three years. Further annual external audits as with other standards (e. g. ISO 27001) are not mandatory. However, if you do, you should mention this in your completed self-assessment catalogue, as this will increase the external auditor's confidence in your ISMS.

Authorized testing service providers

Assessment service providers must be authorized by ENX® in order to carry out official TISAX® assessments. If you register your company in the ENX® portal, you will receive an up-to-date overview of all authorized assessment service providers.

Please note that not all testing service providers are authorized for all test objectives.

If the auditor (assessor) identifies deviations during the external audits (assessments), initiate corrective measures. You document corrective actions as described in Section 1.5.1. In the case of external audits, a *Corrective Action Plan (CAP)* will be requested from you anyway in the event of deviations. You will always receive details of this in the final meeting of an external audit at the latest.

Implementation of the should requirements

The audits carried out are always documented by the respective audit service provider/certification body. Your only task here is to ensure that you actually receive an audit report. As a paying customer, you are entitled to a test report/audit report and should request this if it is not sent to you.

Management can be informed in various ways. It is conceivable that a representative of the management takes part in the final meeting of the external audit. However, management can also be informed verbally by the ISO. However, management must be informed of the results of the external review/external audit at the latest as part of the *management review* (see Section 1.2.1).

1.6 Incident and crisis management

This section deals with the handling of events that threaten information security or have led to actual damage to information security.

1.6.1 To what extent are information security relevant events or observations reported?

Quote from ISA 6.0.3

Potential security events or observations are detected by anyone. It is vital that anyone can and knows when and how to report anything that one has observed and that has potential security implications (observations) or events so that the experts can decide if and how it needs to be handled.

Must

- A definition for a reportable security event or observation exists and is known by employees and relevant stakeholders. The following aspects are considered:
  - Events and observations related to personnel (e.g., misconduct/misbehavior)
  - Events and observations related to physical security (e.g., intrusion, theft, unauthorized access to security zones, vulnerabilities in the security zones)
  - Events and observations related to IT and cyber security (e.g., vulnerable IT-systems, detected successful or unsuccessful attacks)
  - Events and observations related to suppliers and other business partners (e.g., any incidents that can have negative effect on the security of own organization)
- Adequate mechanisms based on perceived risks to report security events are defined, implemented, and known to all relevant potential reporters.
- Adequate channels for communication with event reporters exist.

Should

- A common point of contact for event reporting exists.
- Different reporting channels according to perceived severity exist (i.e., real time communication for significant events/emergencies in addition to asynchronous mechanisms such as tickets or email) are available.
- Employees are obliged and trained to report relevant events.
- Security event reports from external parties are considered.
  - An externally accessible way to report security events exists and is communicated
  - Reaction to security event reports from external parties are defined
- Mechanism to – and information how to – report incidents is accessible by all relevant reporters.
- A feedback procedure to reporters is established.

Additional requirements very high

- Tests and exercises of event and observation reporting are conducted regularly.

Implementation of the mandatory requirements

You create your own definition of an information security event and document it in a guideline.

You also describe in this guideline a standard procedure for dealing with such incidents. This must include in particular: Any user who discovers a suspicious event must report it. It must be specified to whom (e. g. always to the ISO) the incident is to be reported and how it is to be documented.

Due to the outstanding importance of dealing with information security incidents, take this topic into account in your training planning (see Section 2.1.3). In the *training concept* and the training documents used, employees must be familiarized with different types of information security incidents. In particular, this includes the four types explicitly mentioned in the "mandatory requirements": events relating to personnel, physical security, IT and cyber security and suppliers and other business partners.

A standard form can be used to document each information security event (see also Section 1.6.2).

You create a standard form for recording information security incidents. This must contain at least the following "checkpoints":

- Description of the information security event with date
- Notifier of the information security incident
- Description of the existing evidence and where it is stored
- Evaluation of the information security event (this may also include a classification, see info box "What is an event?")
- Indication of whether disciplinary or criminal measures are required
- Indication of whether your own data protection officer must be informed
- Description of whether criminal charges must be filed (also against unknown persons)
- Description of the action being taken
- Description of the feedback to the reporter
- Optional: Classification of the information security event according to a fixed scheme

It is important to actually use this form and fill it out completely. This applies regardless of whether the original report was made internally or by an external organization (e. g. by a business partner). If individual points (e. g. criminal complaint) are not required, this must also be documented.

A form can also be created in a ticket system or in JIRA by configuring the corresponding input fields there.

What is an event?

It would be overkill to document every unsuccessful attack detected and logged by your antivirus software as an information security event or observation.

Here are some examples of typical information security incidents for orientation:

- An employee has lost his access card to the company.
- An employee has opened a suspicious file attachment in an email. It is unclear whether the file was executed.
- Own systems are demonstrably infected by malware.

You can and should find your own definition of what an information security event is for you. The standard does not prescribe a definition here. You are therefore independent of the frequently used distinction between "information security event" and "information security incident".

You also have the option of classifying information security events, for example according to the following scheme:

- Simulation (0)
- No incident (1)
- Reportable observation, no incident (2)
- Event (3)
- Vulnerability (4)
- Incident (5)
- Serious incident (6)

From the audit practice

In ISA audits, you are often expected to provide at least a few examples of information security events from the recent past.

The reason: Auditors often assume that such events occur several times a year in every company. If you do not have any evidence, it may be assumed that you do not have an established process, which can lead to a reduced maturity level (2 instead of 3) in the audit.

Implementation of the should requirements

In addition to the measures already described, you may offer real-time communication for reporting serious information security incidents. This can either be a permanently manned emergency number or a permanently manned chat service via a messenger. Employees should be trained to use this real-time communication only if they suspect a serious information security event. In other cases, asynchronous communication, e. g. by email, is still available.

The procedure for reporting information security incidents and reportable observations is documented and made available to all employees. In addition, you determine which external bodies (e. g. certain business partners) could report. You set up a reporting channel for these external bodies and inform them of this.

Implementation of additional requirements for "very high" protection requirements

You define a procedure and apply it by regularly practicing how to deal with security incidents.

One simple way to do this is to send simulated phishing emails to your employees. You can commission service providers to do this. The service providers will also provide you with analyses of your employees' user behavior, such as information on how often suspicious links within the emails were clicked on. They will also analyze whether and to what extent employees have reported such suspicious emails. The planned sending of fake phishing emails for training purposes is also sometimes viewed critically, as it can create a negative attitude among employees. As it is a frequently used method, it is presented here. It is up to you to decide whether you want to use it; the standard does not prescribe a specific method.

Another option is to simulate information security incidents. You plan these first, e. g. in the central action planning for your ISMS. Example of a simulated event: Loss of a notebook belonging to a department head on a business trip. The simulated event is documented and then the handling of the event, including response times, is analyzed.

1.6.2 To what extent are reported security events managed?

Quote from ISA 6.0.3

Once security events are reported, it is vital that the handling of the events is managed. This means to ensure that the type and criticality of the reported event as well as the persons responsible are quickly identified to ensure that time-critical aspects can be handled in time. Once identification is done, ensuring that the responsible persons become aware and deal with the event within a reasonable time frame is necessary. Furthermore, if the event affects multiple different persons, or management also include coordinating communication is an important part of event management. Finally, if there are external (contractual or regulatory) reporting requirements, it's important to ensure that these are also fulfilled in a professional way.

Must

- Reported events are processed without undue delay.
- An adequate reaction to reported security events is ensured.
- Lessons learned are incorporated into continuous improvement.

Should

- During processing, reported events are categorized (e.g. by responsibility into personnel, physical and cyber), qualified (e.g. not security relevant, observation, suggested security improvement, security vulnerability, security incident) and prioritized (e.g. low, moderate, severe, critical).
- Responsibilities for handling of events based on their category are defined and assigned. The following aspects are considered:
  - Coordination of incidents and vulnerabilities across multiple categories
  - Qualification and resources
  - Contact mechanisms based on type and priority (e.g., non-time-critical communication, time-critical communication, emergency communication)
  - Absence-management
- A strategy for filing official reports and searching prosecution of potentially criminally relevant aspects of security incidents exists.

Additional requirement high

- Maximum response times based on class, category and severity are defined.
- Event not processed appropriately according to their priority are escalated.
  - Conditions and thresholds such as maximum reaction times before escalation are defined
  - Mechanisms, processes, and contacts for escalation are defined
  - Escalation paths up to the organization's top management is defined
- Lawful, regulatory, and contractual reporting obligations and respective contact information are known.
- A communication strategy for security related events exist. The following aspects are considered:
- To whom to communicate (e.g., shareholders, affected business partners and customers, other stakeholders, general public)
  - When to communicate
  - Responsibilities for communication
  - Authorization and approval of communication
  - Legal and regulatory restrictions of communication
  - What to communicate (e.g. prepared templates and building blocks for specific scenarios)
  - How to communicate (e.g., communication channels)
  - Procedures for response to supplier security incidents are established. The following aspects are considered:
  - Analysis of the impact on the own organization and invocation of appropriate internal mechanisms
  - The need for reporting according to own reporting procedures

Additional requirement very high

- Handling of events in different categories and priorities is regularly tested.
  - Exercise or simulation of rarely occurring categories and priorities
  - Exercise or simulation include escalation mechanisms

Implementation of the mandatory requirements

Reported security incidents must be processed without unnecessary delay and responded to appropriately. The experience gained in the process should be channeled into continuous improvement.

Expand your described *incident handling* procedure and define responsibilities for handling incidents. Ideally as a team (Computer Emergency Response Team (CERT)) consisting of ISO, IT, data protection officer and management representative to enable incidents to be handled from different perspectives as well as on a deputy basis.

Your approach should be expanded to include response and solution lists that are derived from the actual business requirements, such as the reporting deadlines agreed with customers.

The CERT team should meet regularly (typically quarterly) to incorporate past events and incidents into the continuous improvement process. These meetings should be documented in the action plan.

Implementation of the should requirements

Security incidents should be categorized and prioritised to enable proper handling and communication to interested parties and authorities.

The classification from Section 1.6.1 can be used here to define and document maximum response times for each classification, i.e. severity of the incident.

Here, it can be helpful to document any reasons for the response time (i.e. legal obligations in regulated areas or requirements from contracts) in the same place in order to obtain a central overview for deriving the response and to be able to view all possible reporting obligations in a central location.

Incidents that are not processed on time must be escalated. Ideally, this is done automatically, e. g. by storing the necessary deadlines in the ticket system such as JIRA.

In larger organizations with 100 to 150 employees or more, it is advisable to further define responsibilities depending on the classification of the incident so that top management is only involved in serious incidents.

The reporting obligations to be complied with can be documented as part of the documented external requirements, for example in the format shown in Table 1.6.

Table 1.6 Documentation of reporting obligations (example)

Title	Summary	In case of change	Responsible	
Reporting of security incidents within 72 hours	A security incident must be reported "to Example" if information or data "from Example" could be affected.	Name: Max Mustermann Telephone: E-mail: *Max.Mustermann@Example.com*	ISO, CERT	1.3.
Reporting a security incident within 48 hours	A security incident must be reported to Muster GmbH if information or data from Muster GmbH could be affected.	Name: Erika Musterfrau Telephone: E-mail: *Erika.Mustermann@Exmaple-GmbH.com*	ISO, CERT	1.3.

Implementation of additional requirements for "very high" protection requirements

The CERT meetings should be used to plan simulations of incidents of exceptional severity, analogous to Section 1.6.1.

This means, above all, testing the aspects of (automatic) escalation, but also the corresponding communication (e. g. emergency telephone number to reach the CERT).

1.6.3 To what extent is the organization prepared to handle crisis situations?

Quote from ISA 6.0.3

A crisis situation occurs If exceptional situations (e.g. natural disasters, physical attacks, pandemics, exceptional social situations, cyber-attacks causing major infrastructure failures) are severely disrupting key business operations. In such cases, the main priority of the organization is to handle the situation as gracefully as possible and recover as quickly as possible. To achieve that and since time is of the essence, switching to a crisis management mode executing pre-planned procedures having specific distribution of responsibilities and structures enables an organization to deal with such a situation is the usual approach.

Must

- An appropriate planning to react to and recover from crisis situations exists.
  - The required resources are available.
- Responsibilities and authority for crisis management within the organization are defined, documented, and assigned.
- The responsible employees are defined and qualified for their task.

Should

- Methods to detect crisis situations are established.
  - General indications for the existence or imminence of a crisis situation and specific predictable crisis are identified
- A procedure to invoke and/or escalate crisis management is in place.
- Strategic goals and their priority in crisis situations are defined and known to relevant personnel. The following aspects are considered:
  - Ethical priorities (e.g., protection of life and health)
  - Core business processes (e.g., processes that ensure the survival of the organization)
  - Appropriate information security
- A crisis management team is defined and approved. The following aspects are considered:
  - Management commitment
  - Composition (e.g., participation of all major functions of the organization including organization leadership (management board), business operations (production), HR, information security, corporate security, corporate emergency services, IT/cyber security, communication, finance)
  - Structure and roles
  - Competences of members
  - Expectation and authority
  - Decision making procedures
- Crisis policies and procedures are defined and approved. The following aspects are considered:
  - Exceptional authorities and decision-making processes beyond the crisis management team
  - Primary and backup means of communication
  - Emergency operating procedures
  - Exceptional organizational structures (e.g., reporting, information gathering, decision making)
  - Exceptional functions, responsibilities, and authority (including reporting)
  - Exceptional tools
- Crisis planning is reviewed and updated regularly.

Additional requirement high

- Relevant different potential crisis scenarios are identified. The following aspects are considered:
  - Crisis situations with unavailability of key personnel (e.g. Health crisis, Kidnapping/accidents affecting organization leadership):
  - Crisis situations with unavailable of key physical resources (e.g. fire or natural disasters at specific sites)
  - Crisis situations with outage of key infrastructure (e.g. outage of key communication channels, complete outage of IT infrastructure)

- Necessary resources and information to handle crisis (e.g. communication infrastructure, availability of necessary information such as contact information and relevant risks in different crisis situations) are identified.
  - Appropriate measures to ensure availability of infrastructure or fallback planning and information considering different crisis scenarios are in place
- A communication strategy for crisis situations exist. The following aspects are considered:
- To whom to communicate (e.g., shareholders, affected business partners and customers, other shareholders, general public)
  - When to communicate
  - Responsibilities for communication
  - Authorization and approval of communication
  - Legal and regulatory restrictions of communication (e.g., stock corporation regulations)
  - What to communicate (e.g. prepared templates for statements, contact information and building blocks for specific scenarios)
  - Communication channels (e.g., Media channels, social media)
  - Instruments to monitor communication
  - Instruction and procedures for employees (in case of direct communication approaches such as direct contact of employees by business partners)
- The efficiency, feasibility, and appropriateness of the crisis planning is evaluated regularly.
- Spot based testing of crisis planning is conducted (e.g., simulation, table-top-exercises involving key personnel)

Additional requirement very high

- Crisis exercises and simulations involving all relevant persons, decision makers are conducted regularly.

A crisis situation occurs when exceptional events such as natural disasters, pandemics or major cyberattacks have a significant impact on important business processes. The organization should therefore take measures to ensure the continuous operation of key services and processes.

Implementation of the mandatory requirements

Crisis situations are planned accordingly, and responsibilities and procedures are defined for potential cases.

For small and medium-sized companies, handling these special situations using the same structures as in Section 1.6.1 and Section 1.6.2 is conceivable (CERT team) and common practice. Expand your procedure description accordingly.

In larger organizations with more than 150 employees or an existing crisis management process, this task should be assigned to a team that is less technically oriented and closer to management.

Example pandemic

A pandemic like corona differs from a normal security problem in its far-reaching and long-term impact on all aspects of business life.

While normal security problems are often limited to IT systems and can be resolved quickly, a pandemic affects the health of employees, supply chains and the entire economy.

It requires comprehensive measures such as home office regulations, hygiene protocols and flexible working hours. In addition, companies need to plan not only their IT security, but also their physical security and business continuity. These comprehensive and long-term adjustments require far-reaching strategic and financial decisions compared to dealing with acute incidents.

Implementation of the should requirements

Your organization should be able to quickly identify, process and update its potential major incidents and crises to ensure your team knows what to do to keep the business running safely and smoothly.

Expand your *incident handling* procedure description to include a chapter on "Exceptional events and crises" and implement it when handling incidents to ensure that your CERT team is aware of the responsibility for recognizing exceptional events. The chapter should include:

- **Recognition:** Ensure that the CERT team gathers additional information on current political, industry and news events and discusses potential situations. Possibly set up a group chat or distribution list where current information can be shared.
- **Rapid activation:** The CERT team should be able to get in touch quickly to assess the situation and initiate the crisis management plan.
- **Mobilization of resources:** Establish that the CERT team is empowered to quickly allocate necessary resources and make extraordinary decisions to manage the crisis.
- **Continuity and recovery:** In the event of a crisis, describe which essential processes should be maintained or quickly restored.
- **Compliance with legal and ethical requirements:** Ensure that all crisis management activities are conducted in strict compliance with legal obligations and ethical considerations.

Implementation of additional requirements for "high" protection requirements

The "standard" crisis scenarios described by the standard (pandemic, fire, natural disaster, IT failure) and other conceivable scenarios should be described and planned in advance.

This includes at least rough process planning, taking into account the communication aspect, including reporting channels, responsibilities and any approvals (e. g. Press releases).

The regular tests and exercises should also include exercises for these standard scenarios (e. g. table-top, discussion of scenarios with the CERT team, etc.) in order to constantly check that the crisis planning is appropriate and up to date.

Implementation of additional requirements for "very high" protection requirements

The planned simulations and tests of crisis situations should be expanded to include all relevant persons and provide a complete picture of the adequacy of the planning (not just random samples).

At our discretion, this may also involve the customer's employees in order to map any situations affecting the customer (supply chain disruptions, IT failures).

2
Human Resources

2.1 Personnel management

2.1.1 To what extent is the qualification of employees for sensitive work fields ensured?

Quote from ISA 6.0.3

Competent, reliable and trustworthy employees are a key to information security within the organization Therefore, it is important to check the qualifications of potential employees (e.g. applicants) to an appropriate extent.

Must

- Sensitive work fields and jobs are determined.
- The requirements for employees with respect to their job profiles are determined and fulfilled.
- The identity of potential employees is verified (e.g. checking identity documents).

Should

- The personal suitability of potential employees is verified by means of simple methods (e.g. job interview).
- An extended suitability verification depending on the respective work field and job is conducted. (e.g. assessment center, psychological analysis, checking of references, certificates and diploma, checking of certificates of conduct, checking of professional and private background).

Implementation of the mandatory requirements

Identification of sensitive positions

You must be able to identify positions and areas of activity that are particularly critical for your organization and have access to particularly confidential information. It is helpful to categorize all positions accordingly. For example:

- Management and authorized signatories
- IT management
- Management
- Employees with special access rights
- Field of activity: IT administration
- Field of activity: Accounting

Ideally, the criticality of the positions should be taken from the *organization chart* (e. g. by position in the hierarchy).

Requirements and verification of identity

The selection of employees should be based on a job profile and the suitability for the job should be verifiable on the basis of the application, the interview and the relevant references.

The identity of employees should be verified upon hiring by presenting their ID card.

Personnel checklist (examples)

The points described here and other points in Section 2.1.1 should be taken into account when hiring, changing or leaving employees.

Ideally, create a checklist for the necessary steps or map them in your HR software, for example, in order to ensure and be able to prove that they have been carried out.

Checklist recruitment procedure	
To do	**Carried out on?**
The applicant fulfils the requirements of the job description (proof of relevant school and vocational training)	
The authenticity of the employee's identity was verified using the ID card	
Check of police clearance certificate (for appointments at management level)	
Personnel file was created	

Checklist recruitment procedure	
First working day	**Carried out on?**
Operational briefing carried out	
Employees are trained in information security issues	
Employees are informed about the sanctions that follow non-compliance with the information security guidelines	
Employees have been committed in writing to information security rules	
Employees were sworn to secrecy in writing (NDA).	

Checklist for extended absences (e. g. Parental leave)	
To do	**Carried out on?**
An e-mail was sent to the IT department to deactivate the accounts and accesses	

Checklist change of division	
To do	**Carried out on?**
An e-mail was sent to the IT department to deactivate the accounts and accesses and to adjust accesses according to the new activity	

Exit checklist	
To do	**Carried out on?**
All keys have been returned	
An e-mail has been sent to the IT department with the employee's name and the date of departure so that the user account can be deactivated and access rights revoked	
The employee was informed that the non-disclosure agreement applies beyond the employment relationship	

Implementation of the should requirements

Personal suitability

Employees should be checked for personal suitability (integrity, trustworthiness) as part of the recruitment process. Ideally, include the future line manager in the recruitment interviews.

Extended audit

In addition, critical points, as defined in the mandatory requirements, should be subjected to an extended check. For example, the following would be conceivable:

- Verification of the authenticity of certificates of good conduct
- Inspection of police clearance certificates for employees with power of attorney
- Perception of assessment center offers

The checks to be carried out depending on the job criticality should be documented in the *personnel checklist* (Table 2.1).

Table 2.1 Personnel checklist (example)

Example: extended check according to the criticality of the job	Template ID card	Certificate of good conduct check	Checking references	Assessment center
All employees	X			
Managers	X	X		
IT management	X	X	X	
CEO and authorized signatory	X	X	X	X

It may make sense to repeat these checks at regular intervals (such a procedure should first be reviewed under labor law). For example, the certificates of good conduct of all managers can be routinely checked every three years. All checks carried out should be documented.

2.1.2 To what extent is all staff contractually bound to comply with information security policies?

Quote from ISA 6.0.3

Organizations are subject to legislation, regulations and internal policies. Already when hiring staff, it must be ensured that employees commit to compliance with the policies and are aware of the consequences of misconduct.

Must

- An appropriate planning to react to and recover from crisis situations exists.
    - The required resources are available
- Responsibilities and authority for crisis management within the organization are defined, documented, and assigned.
- The responsible employees are defined and qualified for their task.

Should

- A non-disclosure obligation beyond the employment contract or order is in effect.
- Information security aspects are considered in the employment contracts of the staff.
- A procedure for handling violations of said obligations is described.

Implementation of the mandatory requirements

Commitments

As part of the recruitment process, your employees must be obliged to maintain confidentiality (NDA). The non-disclosure agreement should include the non-disclosure of business secrets within the scope of employment. The confidentiality agreement should be signed and filed in the personnel file.

Employees must also be committed to your information security regulations. It is a good idea to obtain written confirmation of compliance with the security regulations as part of the information security training or at the time of employment.

Both points should be taken into account in the *personnel checklist*.

Implementation of the should requirements

Period of validity

Make sure that the non-disclosure agreement is valid beyond the contractual relationship. Ideally, there should be no time limit. A corresponding formulation should be clearly identifiable in the audit.

Information security in the employment contract

The obligation to comply with information security rules should be signed as part of the employment contract. Alternatively, instead of a separate document, a corresponding passage can also be included directly in the employment contract.

Sanctions

If employees, consciously or unconsciously, violate rules, sanctions should be implemented. These procedures should be documented – ideally in the *information security policy*.

The regulation should be graduated – based on the severity of the offences.

Exemplary:

- In the event of unintentional breaches, the Information Security Officer (ISO) will provide follow-up training.
- Disciplinary measures are implemented in consultation with the line manager in the event of deliberate offences.
- The employment relationship will be terminated in the event of repeated offences.
- In the case of particularly serious and deliberate offences, a complaint will be made.

2.1.3 To what extent is staff made aware of and trained with respect to the risks arising from the handling of information?

Quote from ISA 6.0.3

If the requirements and risks of information security are not known to the employees, there is a risk of misconduct resulting in damage to the organization. Therefore, it is important that information security is internalized and practiced as a natural part of their work.

Must

- Employees are trained and made aware.

Should

- A concept for awareness and training of employees is prepared. As a minimum, the following aspects are considered:
  - Information security policy
  - Reports of information security events
  - Reaction to occurrence of malware
  - Policies regarding user accounts and login information (e.g. password policy)
  - Compliance issues of information security
  - Requirements and procedures regarding the use of non-disclosure agreements when sharing information requiring protection
  - Use of external IT services
- Target groups for training and awareness measures (i.e., people working in specific risk environments such as administrators, employees having access to

customer networks, personnel in areas of manufacturing) are identified and considered in a training concept.

- The concept has been approved by the responsible management.
- Training and awareness measures are carried out both at regular intervals and in response to events.
- Participation in training and awareness measures is documented.
- Contact persons for information security are known to employees.

Implementation of the mandatory requirements

Employee training

Employees must be trained in information security issues. Schedule basic information security training in the *action plan* at least once a year.

Also ensure that newly hired employees are trained promptly. You can ensure this by making a corresponding entry in the onboarding checklist.

Implementation of the should requirements

Training concept

Create a *training concept* document in which the basic requirements for your training courses are documented and defined. This includes

- **The topics of your basic training:** The training concept should describe the relevant topics for each type of training that you define. The basic training should contain at least the basic topics required by the standard (guidelines, reporting incidents, behavior in the event of malware, correct technical use of the systems (e. g. regular connection to the company network when not in use to enable updates), handling passwords, compliance & data protection, handling licenses & copyright, confidentiality, use of cloud services). The contact details of the ISO should be referred to again in the basic training.
- **Target group-orientated:** In addition to the basic training, you can define further training courses that cover specific areas of work (e. g. Development, IT, HR). Here, too, the relevant key topics should be described in the training concept.
- **Reason-related follow-up training:** In addition to the special training courses, reason-related follow-up training should also be provided, which can be used, for example, to make employees aware of the applicable guidelines once again in the event of repeated incidents.

Participation

Participation in training courses should be documented (e. g. classic list of participants, screenshot of video conference participant list).

On-site or online training?

Various formats are conceivable for training courses. For example, on-site training, live training via video conference or recorded training in conjunction with an online knowledge test.

The standard does not specify a format; you are free to decide how you want to organize training courses. Table 2.2 shows some examples.

Table 2.2 Different training options (examples)

Designation	Method	Frequency	Responsible	Target group
Basic information security training and prototype protection module	Seminar	Annually	ISO	All employees
Secure software development	External seminar	Every two years	IT management	Software development
Current dangers on the net	Newsletter	Monthly	ISO	All employees
Retraining	Seminar	As required	ISO	Employees affected

2.1.4 To what extent is mobile work regulated?

Quote from ISA 6.0.3

Working outside the specifically defined security zones (teleworking) creates risks requiring corresponding protective measures.

Must

- The requirements for teleworking are determined and fulfilled. The following aspects are considered:
    - Secure handling of and access to information (in both electronic and paper form) while considering the protection needs and the contractual requirements applying to private (e.g. home office) and public surroundings (e.g. during travels)
    - Behavior in private surroundings
    - Behavior in public surroundings
    - Measures for protection from theft (e.g. in public surroundings)
- The organization's network is accessed via a secured connection (e.g. VPN) and strong authentication.

Should

- The following aspects are considered:
  - Measures for travelling (e. g. viewing by authorities)
  - Measures for travelling to security-critical countries
- Employee awareness.

Additional requirements high

- Protective measures against overhearing and viewing are implemented. (C)

Implementation of the mandatory requirements

Requirements for mobile working

Define a *mobile working policy* to set out the applicable rules and communicate them to employees. This can also be supplemented with basic operational aspects and rules of conduct for mobile working in the company. The following aspects must be regulated for the standard:

- It should not be possible for unauthorized persons to view confidential information. This includes, for example, a ban on processing confidential information in public places. Compare these rules once again with the *information classification policy*. The use of paper documents for mobile working should be avoided as far as possible.
- The specific types of information that may be processed in public spaces (cafés, means of transport) and private spaces (home office, hotel rooms) should be regulated.
- It should be specifically defined how an employee is to protect equipment from theft when travelling (e. g. devices should not be left unattended if possible).

Network access

In addition, you should ensure that access to company resources only takes place via secure connections (VPN, HTTPS) and that there is therefore protection against threats in public networks (WLAN in trains, private homes).

Implementation of the should requirements

Inspection by authorities

Specific rules should be established for cross-border travel activities that employees must follow when planning and travelling. It is advisable to define specific steps ("travel checklist") for countries or groups of countries that are regularly travelled to, which are anchored in the *mobile working policy*.

Rules do not necessarily have to be drawn up for countries or groups of countries that you do not travel to regularly.

However, to ensure that future travel does not take place without prior assessment, the *mobile working policy* should require approval by ISO and management when travelling to country groups that have not yet been defined.

Co-operation with authorities

When travelling to countries outside the EU, it is to be expected that devices will be confiscated and searched. Data may also be copied in the process. Encryption is not conclusively protective: It may not always be permissible to hand over the password, but officials may still demand it (under pressure).

The devices should be prepared accordingly before travelling and cleared of sensitive data. *Password Manager*, for example, offers a travel mode in which data is removed from the local device. This can be deactivated again on arrival. It is also conceivable to block access for the duration of the journey and only release it again once the employee has made contact. If there is a suspicion that the device has been compromised, the device can also remain blocked until it has been analyzed.

Employees should be reminded of the existing protective measures before travelling. In any case, for the safety of your employees, it is advisable to fully co-operate with border officials and to be technically equipped against possible dangers.

The regulations on travelling should also be compared once again with local laws, particularly with regard to cryptography (Section 5.1.1). Relevant legal norms of countries regularly travelled should be taken into account in the legal cadaster (Section 7.1.1).

Special case of workation

If employees in your company also have the opportunity to work abroad temporarily, you should ensure that you also apply the rules described. From an information security perspective, it makes no difference whether a trip is for business purposes or whether the employee is on a work trip.

Ideally, you should oblige your employees to inform you of the destination country so that the country-specific risks and legal requirements (e.g. on the maximum length of stay) can be checked.

Implementation of additional requirements for "high" protection requirements

Protection against eavesdropping and inspection

The *guideline on mobile working* should be expanded to include specific rules of behavior that make eavesdropping and inspection more difficult. This includes

- The processing of confidential information only if access by third parties can be ruled out.
- Conducting confidential conversations only in closed rooms.
- The use of privacy screens when travelling.

3 Physical Security

3.1 Physical security and business continuity

3.1.1 To what extent are security zones managed to protect information assets?

Quote from ISA 6.0.3

Security zones provide physical protection of information assets. The more sensitive the information assets to be processed are the more protective measures are required.

Must

- A security zone concept including the associated protective measures based on the requirements for the handling of information assets is in place:
  - Physical conditions (e.g. premises/buildings/spaces) are considered in the definition of security zones
  - This also includes delivery and shipping areas
- The defined protective measures are implemented.
- The code of conduct for security zones is known to all persons involved.

Should

- Procedures for allocation and revocation of access rights are established.
- Visitor management policies (including registration and escorting of visitors) are defined.
- Policies for carrying along and using mobile IT devices and mobile data storage devices (e.g. registration before they are carried along, identification obligations) are defined and implemented.

- Network/infrastructure components (own or customer networks) are protected against unauthorized access.
- External properties used for storing and processing information assets are considered in the security zone concept (e.g. storage rooms, garages, workshops, test tracks, data processing centers).

Additional requirements high

- Protective measures against simple overhearing and viewing are implemented. (C)

Implementation of the mandatory requirements

Definition of a security zone concept

To implement a security zone concept, it is advisable to define an *access policy.*

Define various security zones in such a document. The following are common and recommended:

- **White zone:** for public areas such as driveways, car parks and vestibules
- **Green zone:** a zone for internal premises, but where no sensitive information is processed
- **Yellow zone:** a zone for rooms with processes requiring protection such as offices, construction rooms or production areas
- **Red zone:** a zone for rooms with special protection requirements such as server rooms, storage rooms for prototypes or offices of particularly sensitive locations

Appropriate protective measures must be defined, assigned and implemented for each of these zones. This includes, among other things

- The use of a locking system to secure the rooms
- Video surveillance (e. g. for delivery areas or access to red zones)
- The use of an alarm system
- Rules for taking visitors into the respective zones

Assign these protective measures to the respective zones. A typical zone definition, based on the recommendations of the VDA, is shown in Table 3.1.

The *access guideline* should include a floor plan showing the respective color assignments ("Which room belongs to which zone?").

The measures and rules defined in this section should be communicated to employees as part of *information security training*.

Table 3.1 Zone definition (example)

Zone	White (public)	Green (controlled zone)	Yellow (restricted zone)	Red (high-risk zone)
Explanation	Areas with a public character (permanently or temporarily freely accessible to everyone). Low-risk areas without sensitive assets. No or preventive security requirements. Domestic authority exists (e.g. Visitor car park).	Area with technical or organizational security measures. Not freely accessible. Usually internal perimeters.	Area with additional security measures. Restrictive. Protection of special scopes, limited number of persons and usually also confidential scopes.	Area with the highest security requirements. Protection of highly sensitive assets. Strictly regulated access authorizations, usually also strictly confidential scopes.
Visibility	...	...	...	...
Visitor specifications	...	...	...	...
...	...	...	...	...

Implementation of the should requirements

Physical access authorizations

The allocation of access and locking authorizations should be explicitly described. It is advisable to add a formal procedure to the *physical access policy* that describes this:

- Which roles in the company have access to which rooms or room groups?
- How and when are keys and transponders created and issued?
- If a key or transponder is lost, what steps are taken to revoke access authorizations?
- How are access authorizations adjusted in the event of a change of role?
- How are access authorizations withdrawn when an employee leaves the company?

The granting and withdrawal of these access authorizations should also be taken into account in the *personnel checklist*.

Visitors

Expand the *physical access policy* to include a section that explicitly describes how to deal with visitors. This includes the following regulations:

- Visitors should be registered in a visitor list in order to be able to track which people have been in the company and when.
- Visitors should show their ID when they are added to the visitor list.
- Visitors should only be guided through the company under escort. Exceptions are conceivable for white and green zones, but these should be evaluated as part of the *risk assessment*.

The zone-related rules from the mandatory section should also be supplemented with visitor-related aspects:

- Can visitors be taken into the respective zone?
- Travelling in yellow and red zones should only take place in exceptional cases under certain conditions (e. g. Fitters under escort).

Mobile devices

Expand the visitor regulations to include specific aspects on the use of mobile devices for fulfilment:

- The Internet and network should only be used via a separate guest network.
- The use of devices in sensitive zones (yellow and red) can be prohibited or restricted (e. g. by masking the camera or placing the devices in front of the respective zone).
- In addition, mandatory registration of the devices is conceivable.

Infrastructure protection

The infrastructure on your premises should be protected against unauthorized access. The following aspects should be checked to ensure adequate protection:

- Network sockets, network cables or components should not be accessible in public areas.
- If possible, unused network sockets should be unpatched.
- Devices located in public areas (e. g. computers in the entrance or delivery area) must be protected (e. g. by locking them in a cage) so that unauthorized persons cannot access ports.

External properties

For fulfilment, you should ensure that the security zones are also applied to external premises such as warehouses or workshops.

This also includes rented premises in the data center; the level of protection here is generally also very high. Formal attention must nevertheless be paid to assigning these premises to the red zone.

Implementation of additional requirements for "high" protection requirements

Protection against eavesdropping and viewing

You should ensure that it is not easy to view or listen in.

For example, if you have office windows facing a busy street, the screens should not be easily visible from there (e. g. turn the screens round or attach privacy film to the windows).

In addition, employees should be obliged to remove information when leaving the workplace (locking up documents, locking the computer screen) via a *clean desk policy*.

3.1.2 (Replaced)

The chapter has been replaced in ISA 6 by 1.6.3, 5.2.8 and 5.2.9.

3.1.3 To what extent is the handling of supporting assets managed?

Quote from ISA 6.0.3

During their lifecycle (e.g. usage, disposal), supporting assets are subject to risks such as loss, theft or unauthorized viewing.

Must

- The requirements for the handling of supporting assets (e.g. transport, storage, repair, loss, return, disposal) are determined and fulfilled.

Additional requirements high

- Supporting assets are protected. Disposal of supporting assets is conducted in accordance with one of the relevant standards (e.g. ISO 21964, at least Security Level 4). (C)

Implementation of the mandatory requirements

Review your *information classification policy* created in 1.3.2. The policy should contain rules on the use of information carriers for each classification level. This concerns rules on:

- Transport: Can the respective information carrier (e. g. notebook with confidential documents) be transported outside the company? What measures must be observed?
- Storage: What rules apply with regard to storage?
- Returns: What rules need to be observed when returning goods?

Implementation of additional requirements for "high" protection requirements

Check your *disposal policy*.

The disposal of data carriers with confidential content should be carried out at least in accordance with ISO 21964 level 4. This means that

- Check shredders in the company; these should fulfil the standard.
- Alternatively: Hire a data destruction company to shred the collected paper documents for you.
- Disposed digital data carriers should also be disposed of in accordance with this standard. Standard data destruction providers also offer this service.
- Alternatively, a secure overwriting or discarding of the cryptographic key (e. g. by resetting the TPM module) is also conceivable for encrypted media.

The procedure for disposing of paper and digital data carriers should be described in the *disposal policy*.

3.1.4 To what extent is the handling of mobile IT devices and mobile data storage devices managed?

Quote from ISA 6.0.3

Mobile IT devices (e. g. notebooks, tablets, smartphones) and mobile data storage devices (e. g. SD cards, hard drives) are generally used not only on the premises of an organization, but also in mobile applications. This presents an increased risk with respect to e. g. loss or theft.

Must

- The requirements for mobile IT devices and mobile data storage devices are determined and fulfilled. The following aspects are considered:
  - Encryption
  - Access protection (e. g. PIN, password)
  - Marking (also considering requirements for use in the presence of customers)

Should

- Registration of the IT devices.
- Users are informed of missing data protection on mobile devices.

Additional requirements high

- General encryption of mobile data storage devices or the information assets stored thereon:
  - Where this is technically not feasible, information is protected by similarly effective measures

Implementation of the mandatory requirements

Mobile devices and data carriers should be adequately protected.

Ensure that mobile devices (smartphones, notebooks) and mobile data carriers are encrypted by IT. This includes, for example, using Bitlocker under Windows or setting a PIN under iOS to activate encryption.

If it is not possible to encrypt data carriers, a *risk assessment* must be carried out for the respective situation.

Also check whether the mobile IT devices and data carriers should be labelled. This is not normally necessary for mobile IT devices, as a serial number is already affixed to the housing. In the case of mobile data carriers such as external removable hard drives or USB sticks, labelling on the housing may be useful, e. g. to avoid confusion.

Implementation of the should requirements

All IT devices should be registered centrally so that they can be tracked, and the applicability of security requirements can be checked.

You can fulfil this, for example, by

- Inclusion of the devices in the Active Directory
- Registration of devices in a mobile device management system
- Registration of devices in endpoint protection management

In the *information security training*, make sure that employees are informed that end devices are not included in the data backup. Data should therefore be backed up to central systems promptly to prevent data loss.

Implementation of the additional requirements for "high" protection requirements

These requirements have already been met by implementing our recommendations on the mandatory requirements.

4 Identity and Access Management

This chapter deals with the control of access to information. This essentially concerns access to electronically stored information, but also to physical spaces.

4.1 Identity management

4.1.1 To what extent is the use of identification means managed?

Quote from ISA 6.0.3

To check the authorization for both physical access and electronic access, means of identification such as keys, visual IDs, other physical access devices as well as cryptographic tokens are often used. The security features are only reliable if the use of such identification means is handled adequately.

Must

- The requirements for the handling of identification means over the entire life-cycle are determined and fulfilled. The following aspects are considered:
  - Creation, handover, return and destruction
  - Validity periods
  - Traceability
  - Handling of loss

Should

- Identification means can be produced under controlled conditions only.

Additional requirements high

- The validity of identification means is limited to an appropriate period.
- A strategy of blocking or invalidation of identification means in case of loss is prepared and implemented as far as possible.

Implementation of the mandatory requirements

You first determine which physical means of access exist in your company. For access to buildings and rooms, these can be e. g.: keys, tokens or access cards. For access to IT systems, these can be e. g.: physical tokens or cards with magnetic strips.

In the next step, identify and describe the following points (e. g. in the central *information security policy*):

- Where do you obtain the means of access and who can duplicate them (in the case of rented buildings, the landlord often has sovereignty over this; if you own the building yourself, you own the locking system)?
- What is the process for handing over and withdrawing access to your employees?
- How is access equipment that is no longer required destroyed?
- Should validity periods be defined (e. g. Token for door opening is only activated for one year by default, activation must be extended afterwards)?
- What is the process if a means of access is lost? (For example, does the entire locking system have to be replaced if a key is lost?)

Implementation of the should requirements

You also identify and describe the following points, e. g. in an *access policy*:

- Production or duplication is only possible for authorized people. Example: The keys can only be duplicated by a locksmith upon presentation of proof of purchase from the manufacturer. In contrast to keys with a low security level, which can be copied by practically any locksmith.
- Each issue of means of identification is logged. Ideally, each individual means of identification is clearly labelled, e. g. with a unique number.
- There is a process that regulates the timely and recorded return of means of identification.

The above includes being able to provide evidence of the issue and return of means of identification during the audit, e. g. in the form of issue lists with signatures.

Implementation of additional requirements for "high" protection requirements

You also explicitly identify and describe the following points:

- You define validity periods for means of identification (this will only be possible for electronic means of identification, not for keys) and implement them. An "appropriate period" for the duration of validity must always be based on the need to use the means of identification. A means of identification may only be issued for as long as it is required by the respective employee. A "reasonable period" can therefore be the duration of the entire employment relationship or just the duration of a specific project.

- You describe in detail how to block and/or invalidate means of identification in the event of loss. This is not possible for keys. As an alternative, there is a binding procedure for replacing locks/locking systems after a key has been lost.

Special case: Soft tokens

Although Section 4.1.1 is aimed at physical means of identification, we understand that soft tokens are also included in this section. These are also means of access and can be used to access IT systems and rooms.

If you use soft tokens in your company, we therefore recommend that you define and document rules for their use as described.

4.1.2 To what extent is the user access to IT services and IT systems secured?

Quote from ISA 6.0.3

Only securely identified (authenticated) users are to gain access to IT systems. For this purpose, the identity of a user is securely determined by suitable procedures.

Must

- The procedures for user authentication have been selected based on a risk assessment. Possible attack scenarios have been considered (e.g. direct accessibility via the internet).
- State of the art procedures for user authentication are applied.

Should

- The user authentication procedures are defined and implemented based on the business-related and security-relevant requirements:
    - Users are authenticated at least by means of strong passwords according to the state of the art.
- Superior procedures are used for the authentication of privileged user accounts (e.g. Privileged Access Management , two-factor authentication).

Additional requirements high

- Depending on the risk assessment, authentication procedure and access control have been enhanced by supplementary measures (e.g. continuous access monitoring with respect to irregularities or use of strong authentication, automatic logout, disabling in case of inactivity, or brute force prevention).

Additional requirements very high

- Before gaining access to data of very high protection needs, users are authenticated by means of strong authentication (e.g. two-factor authentication) according to the state of the art.

This section deals with access to IT systems: the procedures and standards by which users are able to access IT systems and how unauthorized users are prevented from accessing them.

Implementation of the mandatory requirements

For each individual IT system, you determine which user authentication procedure should be selected. In doing so, consider possible risks – e. g. whether particularly sensitive information is processed in the respective IT system. If you have already created a centralized asset inventory (see Section 1.3.1), you already have an overview of all IT systems. It is a good idea to document the results, including the risks you have taken into account. This is best done in your risk matrix (see Section 1.4.1).

For each procedure that is to be used, you check whether it corresponds to the current state of the art. You can obtain information on this from the German Federal Office for Information Security (BSI) or the specialized media. The current state of the art can refer to requirements for passwords, such as the minimum length and specified special characters.

Implementation of the should requirements

You ensure that privileged user accounts (e. g. of system administrators) are more strongly protected than standard user accounts or those with fewer rights. Alternatively, select a very high level of protection for all user accounts, e. g. by always using two-factor authentication.

Implementation of the additional requirements for "high" protection requirements

Where possible, they use additional protective measures. The standard suggests the following: permanent monitoring of access for irregularities or the use of strong authentication, automatic logout or blocking in the event of inactivity.

To protect against *brute force attacks*, an automatic mechanism is often set up that enforces a time limit after a specified number of incorrect entries until new entries are possible. This is already preset in newer Windows versions, for example (for logging in as a user to Windows). As a company, you can configure the corresponding settings – e. g. permitted number of incorrect entries and duration of the subsequent time limit.

Cloud services often offer protection against *brute force attacks* by using CAPTCHAS or related procedures.

Therefore, check your systems and applications to see whether there is preconfigured protection against *brute force attacks* and whether this is sufficient for your security requirements. If necessary, increase the protection.

Brute force attacks are cyber-attacks in which security barriers are broken through repetitive user password variants based on a system.

Implementation of the additional requirements for "very high" protection requirements

You protect any access to data with very high protection requirements (see Section 1.3.2) with state-of-the-art procedures – e. g. two-factor authentication

4.1.3 To what extent are user accounts and login information securely managed and applied?

Quote from ISA 6.0.3

Access to information and IT systems is provided via validated user accounts assigned to a person. It is important to protect login information and to ensure the traceability of transactions and accesses.

Must

- The creating, changing, and deleting of user accounts is conducted.
- Unique and personalized user accounts are used.
- The use of "collective accounts" is regulated (e.g. restricted to cases where traceability of actions is dispensable).
- User accounts are disabled immediately after the user has resigned from or left the organization (e.g. upon termination of the employment contract).
- User accounts are regularly reviewed.
- The login information is provided to the user in a secure manner.
- A policy for the handling of login information is defined and implemented. The following aspects are considered:
  - No disclosure of login information to third parties
  - Not even to persons of authority
  - Under observation of legal parameters
  - No writing down or unencrypted storing of login information
  - Immediate changing of login information whenever potential compromising is suspected
  - No use of identical login information for business and non-business purposes
  - Changing of temporary or initial login information following the 1st log-in-requirements for the quality of authentication information (e.g. length of password, types of characters to be used).
- The login information (e. g. passwords) of a personalized user account must be known to the assigned user only.

Should

- A basic user account with minimum access rights and functionalities is existent and used.
- Default accounts and passwords pre-configured by manufacturers are disabled (e.g. by blocking or changing of password).
- User accounts are created or authorized by the responsible body.
- Creating user accounts is subject to an approval process (four-eyes principle).
- User accounts of service providers are disabled upon completion of their task.
- Deadlines for disabling and deleting user accounts are defined.
- The use of default passwords is technically prevented.
- Where strong authentication is applied, the use of the medium (e.g. ownership factor) is secure.
- User accounts are reviewed at regular intervals. This also includes user accounts in customers' IT systems.
- Interactive login for service accounts (technical accounts) is technically prevented.

This section deals with the use of user accounts. In particular, the standard requires the use of personalized user accounts.

Implementation of the mandatory requirements

You set up your systems so that each user has their own personalized user account. Collective accounts (e. g. "Production employees") or accounts that are constantly assigned to new people ("interns") should be avoided at all costs.

You create a policy for the provision of user access to IT systems, either as a standalone policy *(access policy)* or as part of the overarching *information security policy*. Here you describe at least the following points:

- The creation, modification and deletion of user accounts follow a defined standard procedure. You define this and ensure that it is applied.
- This standard procedure ensures that personalized user accounts are always blocked immediately after a user leaves the company (e. g. due to a move to another company).
- You regulate the use of collective accounts. These may only be used if no security-relevant settings can be made and/or the "need-to-know principle" is not violated. For example, administrators' access should never be made accessible via a collective account. There should also be no collective accounts for web services that store confidential information on various customers, for example, if this gives employees from outside the project access to customer project data. (Example: a company account for *miro.com* – then every employee would have access to the entire database, even for projects in which they are not involved).

You create a *password policy*. Either as a stand-alone policy or as part of the overarching *information security policy*. Here you describe at least the following points:

- You define the procedure by which login information for the initial login (in particular the initial password) is sent to the respective user. The procedure must be secure, i.e. it must be considerably more difficult for unauthorized persons to obtain the login information. One possible procedure is: delivery in a sealed envelope.
- You stipulate that users must not disclose their login information to anyone – not even to superiors within the company. Exceptions are judicial/official requirements.
- You stipulate that users may neither write down their login information nor store it in unencrypted form. In practice, this means that the familiar "piece of paper on the monitor" is prohibited. This also applies analogously to digital storage: Lists with usernames and passwords may never be stored unencrypted.
- You define and also ensure technically in your IT systems (if technically possible) that the initial password must be changed after the first login.
- You specify that only the respective user may know the respective passwords of their user accounts. This must be ensured through suitable processes and technical settings. Exceptions are possible for the initial password: It may sometimes be necessary to create the password manually and send it to the user. The risk here is low, however, as the initial password must be changed after the user logs in for the first time (see above).
- You define the minimum requirements for password strength (e. g. Minimum length). Please also note business smartphones: You must also set requirements for these. Example: at least a six-digit PIN to unlock the home screen. These minimum requirements should not only be specified in the form of an instruction but should also be enforced technically. To stay with the example of smartphones: If you have Mobile Device Management (MDM), you can technically enforce the minimum requirements here.

Implementation of the should requirements

You use basic user profiles with minimal rights and without group membership. New users are only granted additional rights when there is a specific need.

Check whether the provider of the software used in your company has assigned default passwords. If this is the case, deactivate them.

You technically ensure that no standard passwords are used in your company. This means that every time a new user account is created, or a new password is assigned if a password is lost, a new and individual password is assigned, not a standard password with the same name.

You supplement the guideline for handling login information with the following regulations:

- You determine who in the company is authorized to create user accounts. This can be the IT department or, in smaller companies, the management itself.
- You define a standard procedure so that user accounts that you assign to service providers are blocked again promptly after the service providers have completed their work.
- You determine standard blocking and deletion periods for passwords and also define these technically.
- If you use physical devices for login or authentication (e. g. card readers for smart cards or the electronic ID card), regulate the secure storage when not in use and the authorizations for the use of these devices.
- You specify that user accounts are to be checked regularly, at least once a year. You can schedule this task in the *action plan.*
- Each user should only have the rights they actually need for their work.
- You also check user accounts that have been provided to you by customers for working in their systems.

Implementation of the regular audit

Regular checks can be carried out by the ISO or individual department heads, for example. Ideally, you should always assign this task to a person who does not create user accounts themselves so that the dual control principle is maintained. These checks serve to verify that the assigned user accounts are appropriate and up to date. While missing authorizations are usually quickly noticed as the respective user actively addresses them, there may well be some "skeletons in the closet" – i.e. user rights that were once useful but are no longer needed. These should be uncovered and adapted. The review can also uncover actual security incidents: User authorizations that should not have been granted in the first place.

Depending on the number of employees and the complexity of the IT systems used, user authorizations can also be checked on a random basis. The results of the check must always be documented.

4.2 Access management

4.2.1 To what extent are access rights assigned and managed?

Quote from ISA 6.0.3

The management of access rights ensures that only authorized users have access to information and IT services. For this purpose, access rights are assigned to user accounts.

Must

- The requirements for the management of access rights (authorization) are determined and fulfilled. The following aspects are considered:
  - Procedure for application, verification and approval
  - Applying the minimum ("need-to-know"/"least privilege") principle
  - Access rights are revoked when no longer needed
- The access rights granted for normal and privileged user accounts and technical accounts are reviewed at regular intervals also within IT systems of customers.

Should

- Strategies for authorizing access to information are prepared.
- Authorization roles are used.
- Rights are allocated on a need-to-use basis and according to the role and/or area of responsibility.
- Normal user accounts are not granted privileged access rights.
- The access rights of a user account are adapted after the user has changed (e.g. to another field of responsibility).

Additional requirements high

- The access rights are approved by the responsible internal Information Officer.

Additional requirements very high

- Prevention of unauthorized persons gaining access and information (privileged users):
  - Information is stored in encrypted form at content level (e.g. file level).
  - Where encryption is not feasible, information shall be protected by similarly effective measures.
- Existing access rights are regularly reviewed at shorter intervals (e.g. quarterly).

This section deals with the authorizations that are associated with the user accounts described.

Implementation of the mandatory requirements

You define a standard procedure for granting and withdrawing user authorizations. You document this procedure. You can do this in various ways, for example in an *ac-*

cess management policy, in checklists or as workflows in ticket software. In the case of new employees and when employees leave the company, the process of granting and withdrawing access rights is closely linked to personnel management (see *Personnel checklist* for onboarding, see Section 2.1.1).

In this procedure, you regulate how the granting and revocation of user authorizations are technically checked to ensure the "need-to-know principle" (each person only sees what they really need for their work). You also realize the "least privilege principle" here by only assigning the absolutely necessary rights to users. An example of this: A user only receives read rights for certain files if write rights are not required for them. You regularly check the assigned user authorizations. Proceed as already described in Section 4.1.3.

You stipulate that the technical check is documented when user authorizations are granted, e. g. by the signature of the checking department head in a checklist.

Implementation of the should requirements

You create authorization concepts. However, the standard is not particularly precise in its description of the requirements. We therefore recommend writing at least one overarching authorization concept for all your IT systems, which describes the requirements and implementation from both a functional ("functional authorization concept") and a technical ("technical authorization concept") perspective. You can also create various individual authorization concepts for your individual systems.

When assigning authorizations, you work with roles, e. g. the role "Marketing department employee". Authorizations for the associated position (in this example: clerk in the marketing department) are linked to the role.

You describe how to ensure that user authorizations are adjusted promptly in day-to-day business, for example when an employee changes department.

You ensure that the "need-to-know principle" is adhered to at all times. This also means that normal users are not granted any privileged authorizations (e. g. administrator access).

Implementation of additional requirements for "high" protection requirements

You synchronize the accesses to systems with the asset inventory. Access to systems may only be assigned with the consent of the respective asset manager.

Implementation of additional requirements for "very high" protection requirements

Wherever possible, encrypt files. For files stored on end devices or local servers, it is advisable to encrypt entire drives or the entire storage medium. In the case of cloud storage, the cloud provider often already offers automatic encryption of the data.

Check the assigned user authorizations at least once a quarter (see also Section 4.1.3).

5 IT Security/Cyber Security

5.1 Cryptography

This chapter deals with the requirements and framework conditions for cryptographic procedures. Specifically, the techniques and procedures used for encryption, signature generation and verification as well as authentication procedures.

5.1.1 To what extent is the use of cryptographic procedures managed?

Quote from ISA 6.0.3

When using cryptographic procedures, it is important to consider risks in the field of availability (lost key material) as well as risks due to incorrectly applied procedures in the fields of integrity and confidentiality (poor algorithms/protocols or insufficient key strengths).

Must

- All cryptographic procedures used (e.g. encryption, signature, and hash algorithms, protocols) provide the security required by the respective application field according to the recognized industry standard.
  - To the extent legally feasible

Should

- Preparation of technical rules containing requirements for encryption in order to protect information according to its classification.
- A concept for the application of cryptography is defined and implemented. The following aspects are considered:
  - Cryptographic procedures

  - Key strengths
  - Procedures for the complete lifecycle of cryptographic keys, including generation, storage, archiving, retrieval, distribution, deactivation, renewal, and deletion
- An emergency process for restoring key material is established.

Additional requirements high

- Key sovereignty requirements (particularly in case of external processing) are determined and fulfilled.

The aim of this section of the standard is to review the cryptographic measures used for appropriateness and up-to-datedness, taking into account the legal framework. Furthermore, minimum requirements for cryptography, in particular encryption strengths, should be defined in order to create a verifiably controllable level of security.

Implementation of the mandatory requirements

List all cryptographic procedures used in a central document and also document the algorithms used there, for example the solution used for hard disk encryption and the associated algorithm. In the case of cryptographic measures for VPN, HTTPS etc., the protocol standard should also be documented (e. g. TLS 1.3).

For example: Microsoft Bitlocker, XTS-AES 128-bit

In order to be able to prove that the cryptographic measures are up-to-date and appropriate, you should compare all applied and documented protocols and algorithms with a common recommendation or assessment.

Recommendation of NIST

The NIST recommendation, for example, is worth mentioning here:

https://csrc.nist.gov/projects/cryptographic-standards-and-guidelines

NIST also communicates the expected validity of recommendation in the future. Accordingly, you can already derive future measures for the migration or conversion of your procedures from these "expiry dates".

Please note, however, that cryptographic measures can be categorized as no longer secure enough at an early stage due to new findings or "gaps" that are discovered. You should therefore check the recommendations regularly.

All procedures used should comply with this or another current, trustworthy recommendation or meet or exceed the recommended security level.

In this way, you create an internal set of rules for the minimum requirements for cryptographic measures, which is also harmonized with an expert recommendation.

You must also compare these requirements with the legal framework. This means: Compare these requirements with any restrictions (e. g. in export), but also (minimum) requirements for cryptography and document these in a legal cadaster (see Chapter 7).

Typical use cases for this include sending encrypted emails or providing encrypted files to a customer or subsidiary abroad. Countries that require special attention include China, Iran and Russia.

Attention: Not only Europe

In Europe, there are currently no significant restrictions on the use of cryptography, but rather minimum standards that may even require its use.

However, local restrictions may apply in other countries in which you may operate. This may already apply if you integrate crypto frameworks into an app that is then available in the respective app store.

A helpful overview can be found at: *https://www.gp-digital.org/world-map-of-encryption*

Implementation of the should requirements

To demonstrate how information in the company is cryptographically protected according to its classification, you should ideally implement two measures.

First and foremost, the basic areas of application of cryptography should be described. Ideally, you should combine this with a list of the algorithms used from the above-mentioned mandatory requirements in order to explain where cryptography is generally used and thus protects all processed information. One example of this is the encryption of all notebook hard drives.

In a second step, rules should be documented that are applied depending on the information classification. Check your information classification documentation to add instructions that employees must follow, such as the manual encryption of highly confidential PDF files.

In addition, you should document which rules are applied in your company for the creation, maintenance and destruction of cryptographic keys.

Also consider in the description how cryptographic keys are secured to enable recovery in an emergency. A situation in which you can no longer access cryptographically secured content due to system failure must be avoided.

Questions to be answered (examples)

How are master certificates monitored during their term?

Which programs are permitted for generating private keys?

How are certificates and keys restored in an emergency?

Implementation of additional requirements for "high" protection requirements

When fulfilling the high protection requirement, it should be explained in which cases the sovereignty for keys lies outside the company. Document the root certificates used for this purpose and the responsibility for them. For example, if you obtain cloud services from a provider that does not integrate its own certificates, certificates and trust settings are most likely managed entirely by the provider. In this case, you relinquish control.

5.1.2 To what extent is information protected during transfer?

Quote from ISA 6.0.3

When being transferred via public or private networks, information can in some circumstances be read or manipulated by unauthorized third parties. Therefore, requirements regarding the protection needs of the information must be determined and implemented by taking suitable measures during such transfer.

Must

- The network services used to transfer information are identified and documented.
- Policies and procedures in accordance with the classification requirements for the use of network services are defined and implemented.
- Measures for the protection of transferred contents against unauthorized access are implemented.

Should

- Measures for ensuring correct addressing and correct transfer of information are implemented.
- Electronic data exchange is conducted using content or transport encryption according to the respective classification.
- Remote access connections are verified to possess adequate security features (e.g., encryption, granting and termination of access) and capabilities.

Additional requirements high

- Information is transported or transferred in encrypted form:
  - Where encryption is not feasible, information must be protected by similarly effective measures

Additional requirements very high

- Information is transported or transferred in content-encrypted form.

In order to protect information during transmission through your own and external networks, you should attempt to have an "all-round view" of the communication channels used and permitted.

Implementation of the mandatory requirements

To explain which network services are used to transfer information, you should ideally document permitted transport routes and services that employees are authorized to use as part of the information classification.

In addition, make sure that the communication channels used and your minimum requirements for cryptography (transport encryption) are taken into account in the documentation mentioned in Section 5.1.1. Even if a classification-dependent security level is generally possible, it is recommended that central communication and network channels are always secured to a high level where possible (VPN, email with STARTTLS).

Implementation of the should requirements

To ensure communication with correct addresses, it is advisable to use systems and addressing for sensitive information that prevent incorrect entries as far as possible. In addition to traditional methods, such as maintaining a central address book, it is also possible to send sensitive information in such a way that the recipient is additionally identified.

For example, it would be conceivable not to send sensitive data directly by email, but via a log-in or one-time password-protected link. Email forwarding to the recipient would then not automatically result in unauthorized persons being able to open the file attachment, for example.

In addition to the mandatory requirements, rules should also be drawn up and checked for appropriateness that specify concrete requirements for the classification of data. For example, confidential data should not be sent unencrypted.

In practice

Wherever possible, these rules should be applied automatically and not be based on explicit compliance by employees.

This includes ensuring that transport routes always have a high level of protection wherever possible or that documents automatically receive a data classification that is respected by communication programs.

For example, it is possible to automatically convert a confidential file into a password-protected link when it is sent by e-mail.

Implementation of the additional requirements for "high" protection requirements

To implement this, ensure that data transfers run via encrypted channels. This includes the use of TLS/HTTPS for all services used, the use of transport encryption for

VoIP and also the use of standard transport encryption when using emails without fallback to plain text.

In cases where this is not possible, alternative procedures must be implemented, such as the encryption of individual files before transport.

In order to implement the requirements regarding the verification of remote access connections, it should be ensured that client software features of cryptographically secured connections are checked for typical features (TLS version, certificate validity, OCSP, etc.). In the case of standard software such as browsers, this is usually already provided by the standard, but specialized and niche software should also be configured accordingly.

Implementation of additional requirements for "very high" protection requirements

The standard requires not only the transport but also the content to be encrypted.

For example, it would be conceivable to implement end-to-end encryption when sending emails. If this is not possible due to the other party, you should consider alternatives to sending by email or only send data as personalized links in order to create a comparable level of protection.

You should also check where content encryption can be used, especially when transmitting confidential information.

5.2 Operations security

This section is about the operational security of your entire IT. The individual subsections therefore contain a range of different requirements to promote the secure operation of IT.

5.2.1 To what extent are changes managed?

Quote from ISA 6.0.3

The aim is to ensure that all changes to the organization, business processes and IT systems take information security aspects into account so that these changes do not lead to an unregulated reduction in the level of information security.

Must

- Information security requirements for changes to the organization, business processes, IT systems are determined and applied.

Should

- A formal approval procedure is established.
- Changes are verified and assessed for their potential impact on the information security.
- Changes affecting the information security are subjected to planning and testing.
- Procedures for fallback in fault cases are considered.

Additional requirements high

- Compliance with the information security requirements is verified during and after the changes are applied.

Implementation of the mandatory requirements

Whenever major changes are being considered within your organization, determine the extent to which information security is affected. It is advisable to define this in a separate *change management policy* or in the central *policy on information security* (see Chapter 1) and to keep written records for each planned change. These records must show the extent to which information security is affected by the change and what options for action are available from your perspective.

The question remains: What types of changes should this approach be applied to? In fact, these are all the changes that take place in your organization. The standard refers to changes to “organization, business processes and IT systems”. This means that not only *IT changes* in the classic sense are meant, but also all other major changes.

Change projects relevant to information security (examples)

Example of changes to the organization: An investor from outside the EU wants to buy your company. This may give the investor access to confidential information.

Example of changes to processes: Your company offers consulting services that in future will no longer be carried out exclusively on site, but increasingly via video transmission. In future, data will be exchanged electronically in both directions.

Example of an *IT change*: You intend to completely replace your own physical servers with servers in the cloud of a large provider.

Information security is affected in all of these cases and must therefore be considered.

In the case of *IT changes* in the sense of new acquisitions or further developments of *IT changes*, please also refer to Section 5.3.1. Here you will find further requirements for such *changes*!

Implementation of the should requirements

You add the following points to your internal specifications for change management:

- There is a formal authorization procedure, ideally graded according to the importance/type of change. Management should always be involved in major changes; smaller changes can also be decided by individual employees in IT alone if necessary.
- A detailed examination of the planned change is carried out and the results are evaluated and documented.
- Changes should be tested whenever possible.

Emergency procedures in case the change have to be cancelled or reversed must be considered. A back-up solution should be prepared in good time whenever possible.

Implementation of additional requirements for "high" protection requirements

You also have the status of ongoing *changes* checked regularly so that you can act in good time in the event of errors or new risks.

How do you document *changes*?

In many companies, it is common practice to document changes in JIRA. One of the advantages of this is that workflows can be predefined. Depending on the type of change, a JIRA template with the appropriate processing and approval workflow can then be used.

An alternative is a change register in table form.

5.2.2 To what extent are development and testing environments separated from operational environments?

Quote from ISA 6.0.3

The objective of separating the development, testing and operational environments is to ensure that the availability, confidentiality and integrity of productive data are maintained.

Must

- The IT systems have been subjected to risk assessment in order to determine the necessity of their separation into development, testing and operational systems.
- A segmentation is implemented based on the results of risk analysis.

Should

- The requirements for development and testing environments are determined and implemented. The following aspects are considered:
  - Separation of development, testing and operational systems
  - No development and system tools on operational systems (except those required for operation)
  - Use of different user profiles for development, testing, and operational systems

This section is particularly important for you if you develop software in your company. By separating development, test and production environments, the integrity of productive data ("real data" from ongoing business) and the confidentiality of this productive data (minimizing the use of productive data in software development) should be ensured.

Implementation of the mandatory requirements

You carry out risk assessments for your IT systems with regard to a possible need to separate the environments. These risk assessments are best documented in the risk matrix (see Section 1.4.1). Based on the risk assessments, you decide whether to separate the environments into a production environment, development environment and test environment.

Implementation of the should requirements

You define in detail how the respective environments are to be designed. Among other things, you define the following (and document this – e. g. in the *development policy*):

- Ensure that no development or testing takes place in the production environment (as far as possible).
- Different user profiles must be used in different environments.

5.2.3 To what extent are IT systems protected against malware?

Quote from ISA 6.0.3

The aim is to both technically and organizationally ensure the protection of IT systems against malware.

Must

- Requirements for protection against malware are determined.
- Technical and organizational measures for protection against malware are defined and implemented.

Should

- Unnecessary network services are disabled.
- Access to network services is restricted to necessary access by means of suitable protective measures (see examples).
- Malware protection software is installed and updated automatically at regular intervals (e.g. virus scanner).
- Received files and software are automatically inspected for malware prior to their execution (on-access scan).
- The entire data contents of all systems are regularly inspected for malware.
- Data transferred by central gateways (e.g. e-mail, internet, third-party networks) is automatically inspected by means of protection software:
  - Encrypted connections are considered
- Measures to prevent protection software from being deactivated or altered by users are defined and implemented.
- Case-related staff awareness measures.
- For IT systems operated without the use of malware protection software, alternative measures (e.g. special resilience measures, few services, no active users, network isolation) are implemented.

This section deals with protection against malware of all kinds, e.g. viruses, Trojans and phishing.

Implementation of the mandatory requirements

You determine the essential requirements for protection against malware for your company. In doing so, you consider both the necessary organizational and technical measures (e.g. installation of endpoint protection software on all company notebooks) and implement them.

Ideally, you should describe the key measures in a separate *malware protection policy* or in a separate chapter in the overarching *information security policy* (see Section 1.1.1).

Implementation of the should requirements

You control access to network services: Deactivate network services that are not required. This applies to web servers, for example: Here, certain services (e.g. FTP) are often not required by default. For companies without their own network that only operate a LAN/WLAN, it is advisable to deactivate the WLAN at times when it is not required (e.g. at night) using a timer.

Limit remote access to the required minimum: Only enable remote access when necessary and only for the required ports. You also use firewalls and activate password protection for the WLANs used.

You install endpoint protection software on all potentially vulnerable computers. You activate regular updates or ensure that updates are installed manually in a timely manner.

You set up "On-Access-Scan ", the automatic scanning of received files and programs before they are executed.

You set up a regular check of the entire database. For example, in the form of weekly scans that run regularly at certain times on certain days of the week.

You set up a centralized automatic check of the data transmitted via central gateways (e. g. email gateway), e. g. by means of an appropriately configured firewall.

You ensure that endpoint protection or the associated settings (e. g. automatic updates) cannot be deactivated or changed by users themselves. You can achieve this, for example, by not granting users admin rights on their notebooks.

You ensure that users are sensitized on a case-by-case basis – e. g. after the occurrence of a specific event. It is best to include this in your training concept (see Section 2.1.3).

If you also operate IT systems without virus protection (e. g. PCs for production control that do not have an internet connection), check which alternative protective measures should be taken and implement them. Ideally, you should document the measures taken here in your *malware protection policy* or in the corresponding chapter in your central *information security policy*. Examples of such measures for hardening and increasing resilience, in addition to those already mentioned, include Removing or disabling unneeded hardware interfaces (including unneeded USB ports) or keeping spare devices (redundancy).

Admin rights: a hurdle in audits

The should requirements are indirectly aimed at the issue of user admin rights. In many companies, it is common practice to equip all notebooks and PCs with admin rights. However, this also gives users the opportunity to make settings to the respective antivirus software, which must be excluded in accordance with the standard.

In audits, it is not appreciated if all employees have admin rights. However, this does not necessarily have to lead to a deviation (Deviation: non-compliance with a TISAX requirement identified in the audit, which would result in no or only a temporary TISAX label being awarded)!

If you have computers with admin rights, you should carry out a risk analysis and document this in your risk matrix. If you are an IT company, you could argue here, for example, that all employees are IT specialists and therefore have a high level of awareness of IT security.

Ideally, you should also have suitable analysis software in operation, which automatically notifies you immediately if virus protection has been deactivated on individual computers.

This combination of risk assessment and analysis software is generally accepted in audits.

Ideally, however, you should limit the number of computers with admin rights to a minimum, for example to the computers for developers.

5.2.4 To what extent are event logs recorded and analysed?

Quote from ISA 6.0.3

Event logs support the traceability of events in case of a security incident. This requires that events necessary to determine the causes are recorded and stored. In addition, the logging and analysis of activities in accordance with applicable legislation (e.g. Data Protection or Works Constitution Act) is required to determine which user account has made changes to IT systems.

Must

- Information security requirements regarding the handling of event logs are determined and fulfilled.
- Security-relevant requirements regarding the logging of activities of system administrators and users are determined and fulfilled.
- The IT systems used are assessed regarding the necessity of logging.
- When using external IT services, information on the monitoring options is obtained and considered in the assessment.
- Event logs are checked regularly for rule violations and noticeable problems in compliance with the permissible legal and organizational provisions.

Should

- A procedure for the escalation of relevant events to the responsible body (e.g. security incident report, data protection, corporate security, IT security) is defined and established.
- Event logs (contents and meta data) are protected against alteration. (e.g. by a dedicated environment).
- Adequate monitoring and recording of any actions on the network that are relevant to information security are established.

Additional requirements high

- Information security requirements relevant to the security during the handling of event logs, e.g. contractual requirements, are determined and implemented.
- Cases of access during connection and disconnection of external networks (e.g. remote maintenance) are logged.

Additional requirements very high

- Logging of any access to data of very high protection needs as far as technically feasible and as permissible according to legal and organizational provisions.

This section deals with event logs (log files) from IT systems. Collection, storage and evaluation are to be determined and regulated.

Implementation of the mandatory requirements

If you do not already have one, first get an overview of all the software used in your company and list it. If you have already created an asset inventory for the company (see Section 1.3), use this, as all software used should already be entered here. Consider both *on-premises software* and software operated in the cloud by external providers.

For each software, you assess individually whether event logs need to be recorded and analyzed. You do this both with regard to the activities of "simple" users and with regard to the activities of administrators.

When are event logs required? This may be the case at, for example, if particularly sensitive information is stored or processed in software, meaning that unauthorized access must be avoided at all costs. Services with centralized access should also be taken into account (VPN server, SSO server).

In the next step, you define exactly which types of user and administrator activities require event logs. This can be, for example: an unusually high number of login attempts, unusually large download volumes, any new creation and deletion of users, etc.

The feasibility must then be checked. This is about whether the required log data can be generated with the available resources. This varies greatly from software to software. Some programs offer the generation of log data with "on-board tools", while others require the purchase of additional modules or the programming of individual solutions.

Finally, you specify who should check the log files for anomalies and how often. There are automated solutions that notify you immediately (e. g. by email alert) as soon as there is suspicious activity. However, it is advisable not to rely completely on such automated solutions, but to always have manual checks carried out (e. g. by the ISO). Every manual check must be documented, even if no anomalies are detected. This can be done informally, e. g. by the ISO.

Ideally, you should summarize the results in a matrix that states which activities you want to log for which software and how the evaluation should take place. This description is best summarized in a *logging policy*

If you detect suspicious events, you must react immediately. To do this, you must draw up a procedure description (a few sentences are sufficient) in which you specify to whom the suspicious events are to be reported.

Content policy logging (example)

- Designation
- Description of the
- Evaluation
- Responsibility
- Storage location
- Requirements
- Storage period

Note data protection!

Individual user activities are visible through log files. This allows conclusions to be drawn about the working behavior of individual employees. When deciding which log files to analyze, you should therefore always consult the data protection officer, the works council or a lawyer (depending on the law of your regional jurisdiction). These should also provide recommendations on the maximum permissible retention period for event logs.

Implementation of the should requirements

You specify that suspicious events are always to be treated as an information security event (see Section 1.6.1). This ensures that the suspicious event is documented and evaluated in sufficient detail and that there is a sufficient flow of information (e. g. to customers, authorities or your company's data protection officer if required).

You ensure that the event logs are protected against manipulation. Here again, the implementation depends on the individual case: If the event logs are stored with a cloud provider and access is controlled via user rights, protection is usually sufficient. However, if the event logs are generated as a TXT file, e. g., you should consider saving them in PDF format and storing them on protected drives.

Finally, the last should requirement is to ensure that network activities are considered in addition to user activities in individual IT applications.

Implementation of additional requirements for "high" protection requirements

You check whether there are any other requirements for event logs, such as requirements arising from contracts with your customers. For example, it might be a customer requirement from a project assignment to log certain user activities.

You technically ensure that network connections "from outside" – e. g. for remote maintenance via TeamViewer – are logged. If this is not technically possible for you, you manually log which provider has carried out remote maintenance or similar access using which software, at what times and for what purpose.

Implementation of additional requirements for "very high" protection requirements

You technically ensure that all access to information with a very high protection requirement is logged. To do this, you first access your asset inventory (see Section 1.3.1) to determine the information with a very high protection requirement and the systems in which it is processed.

You then ensure logging within the scope of the technical possibilities. This is only limited by legal provisions, as described in the "Note data protection!" info box in this section.

5.2.5 To what extent are vulnerabilities identified and addressed?

Quote from ISA 6.0.3

Vulnerabilities increase the risk of IT systems being unable to meet the requirements for confidentiality, availability and integrity. Exploitation of vulnerabilities is among the possible ways for attackers to gain access to the IT system or to threaten its operating stability.

Must

- Information on technical vulnerabilities for the IT systems in use is gathered (e.g. information from the manufacturer, system audits, CVS database) and evaluated (e.g. Common Vulnerability Scoring System CVSS)
- Potentially affected IT systems and software are identified, assessed and any vulnerabilities are addressed.

Should

- An adequate patch management is defined and implemented (e.g. patch testing and installation).
- Risk minimizing measures are implemented, as necessary.
- Successful installation of patches is verified in an appropriate manner.

This section deals with the identification of technical vulnerabilities in the IT systems used and the associated patch management.

Implementation of the mandatory requirements

You define ways to keep yourself continuously informed about technical vulnerabilities in your IT systems. Remember that the software manufacturers themselves only realize certain vulnerabilities during operation or that hackers exploit vulnerabilities until they are closed by the manufacturers. Monitoring vulnerabilities is therefore a never-ending task. Your contribution can be, for example, to continuously monitor information from the respective software manufacturers about possible security vulnerabilities or to keep an eye on the specialized press and relevant portals such as *heise.de*.

Act promptly as soon as you become aware of the vulnerabilities.

Depending on the size and complexity of your IT infrastructure, different approaches to patch management are appropriate. In larger IT infrastructures, patch management should be largely automated. Specialized software is available for this, e. g. *Barracuda* or *Matrix 42*. In smaller IT infrastructures, automatic updates must at least be activated for all locally installed software (including operating systems).

Ideally, the software is configured in such a way that users cannot change the security settings. If this is not possible, users should be trained (see training concept, described in Section 2.1.3) that they must not deactivate automatic updates and must accept proposed updates promptly (e. g. at the end of the working day at the latest).

Automatic firmware updates should also be activated for other devices such as WLAN routers or printers.

It is a good idea to briefly describe your approach to this, e. g. in a *patch management policy* or in a chapter in your overarching *information security policy* (see Section 1.1.1).

Implementation of the should requirements

You define and apply rules for patch management in your company. You decide to what extent patches should be applied manually or automatically and to what extent installed patches should be tested. You consider possible risks and define suitable measures (e. g. fallback options).

Figure 5.1 shows an example of patch management regulations.

		Damage potential of the vulnerability		
		Normal	High	Very high
Possible risk due to patch installation	Normal	Patch will be rolled out within 24 hours	Patch will be rolled out within 8 hours	Patch will be rolled out immediately
	High	The patch is tested within 24 hours in the test environment and then rolled out (see Section 2.4)	The patch is tested within 8 hours in the test environment and then rolled out (see Section 2.4)	The patch is tested within 4 hours in the test environment and then rolled out (see Section 2.4)
	Very high	The patch is tested within 48 hours in the test environment and then rolled out (see Section 2.4)	The patch is tested within 24 hours in the test environment and then rolled out (see Section 2.4)	The patch is tested within 4 hours in the test environment and then rolled out (see Section 2.4)

Figure 5.1 Example of patch handling

5.2.6 To what extent are IT systems and services technically checked (system and service audit)?

Quote from ISA 6.0.3

The objective of technical checks is the detection of states which can jeopardize the availability, confidentiality or integrity of IT systems and services.

Must

- Requirements for auditing IT systems or services are determined.
- The scope of the system audit is specified in a timely manner.
- System or service audits are coordinated with the operator and users of the IT systems or services.
- The results of system or service audits are stored in a traceable manner and reported to the relevant management.
- Measures are derived from the results.

Should

- System and service audits are planned to take into account any security risks they might cause (e. g. disturbances).
- Regular system or service audits are performed

   - Carried out by qualified personnel
   - Suitable tools (e.g. vulnerability scanners) are used for system and service audits (if applicable)
   - Performed from the internet and the internal network
- Within a reasonable period following completion of the audit, a report is prepared.

Additional requirements high

- For critical IT systems or services, additional system or service audit requirements have been identified and are fulfilled (e.g., service specific tests and tools and/or human penetration tests, risk-based time intervals)

Additional requirements very high

- IT systems and services are regularly scanned for vulnerabilities.
   - Suitable protective measures must be implemented for systems and services that may not be scanned

---

This section deals with the regular technical inspection of the hardware and software you use.

Implementation of the mandatory requirements

You define a standard procedure to ensure that technical inspections are carried out systematically, safely and in a documented manner. Please also refer to the descriptions in Section 1.5.1.

Use your audit program, audit plans and audit reports for the technical inspections.

You initially determine which IT systems and services are to be technically audited. In doing so, you take known information security risks into account and also review your risk matrix (see Section 1.4.1) and your central inventory of assets (see Section 1.3.1). Once you have determined which systems are to be checked using which methods (e.g. PEN tests, performance tests or other tests), write down the rough planning in your audit program. Please note: You are always free to have individual technical checks carried out by external experts.

In good time before the individual technical audits, create an audit plan containing the details of the planned audit, e.g. Date, location, systems and services involved, test method, responsible persons, etc. You also check whether the audits jeopardize ongoing operations and whether users need to be informed in good time. You also document this in the respective audit plan.

The results of these audits are documented in audit reports. The entire coordination can be carried out by the ISO, but it must be ensured that the company management is sufficiently informed. If major weaknesses or errors are found, the company management should be informed immediately. If the audits are inconspicuous, it may be sufficient for the ISO to report the results to the company management once a year as part of the management review (see Section 1.2.1).

If weaknesses or errors are found, these must always be responded to. Appropriate measures must be introduced and their effectiveness evaluated ("performance review"). The measures and the results of the effectiveness evaluation must be documented in writing.

Implementation of the should requirements

Before each audit, you carry out an analysis of possible disruptions to operations in good time and document the result of this analysis in the audit plan. Depending on the result, you decide on possible measures so that the audit can take place under safe conditions.

You only allow audits to be carried out by sufficiently qualified specialists. In the audit plan, you document what qualifies the planned auditor for the respective audit.

You ensure that the appropriate tools are available for a successful audit, e. g. in the form of analysis software. Which tools these are depends on the type of technical review selected in each individual case.

Implementation of additional requirements for "high" protection requirements

To fulfil these requirements, you first identify the critical IT systems or services. You are free to decide which criteria you use to assess criticality and which IT systems or services you ultimately categorize as critical. In the first step, it is best to use the asset inventory you have already created and the risk matrix you have created to identify potentially critical IT systems and services.

You record the IT systems and services you have identified as critical in your audit program and also document there which types of tests you consider necessary and at what frequency.

Implementation of additional requirements for "very high" protection requirements

In larger IT organizations, vulnerability scans are usually carried out using suitable software and/or by external providers. The reports generated by the software or provided by the external providers can also be used as audit reports. They must therefore be archived in a traceable manner.

In smaller IT organizations without their own network, vulnerability scans can be carried out using endpoint protection software ("antivirus program"). However, such a function is not integrated in every endpoint protection software and the range of functions varies from provider to provider. The reports must also be archived here, e. g. in the form of screenshots.

Remember: In the case of cloud services, vulnerability scans are carried out by the respective provider. When selecting cloud providers (see Section 1.2.4), it is therefore important that you check whether regular vulnerability scans are carried out.

If individual systems or services cannot be scanned, carry out manual checks. For example, check at regular intervals whether the latest software versions are installed. You should also plan and document this in your audit program and in audit reports.

5.2.7 To what extent is the network of the organization managed?

Quote from ISA 6.0.3

IT systems in a network are exposed to different risks or have different protection needs. In order to detect or prevent unintended data exchange or access between these IT systems, they are subdivided into suitable segments and access is controlled and monitored by means of security technologies.

Must

- Requirements for the management and control of networks are determined and fulfilled.
- Requirements regarding network segmentation are determined and fulfilled.

Should

- Procedures for the management and control of networks are defined.
- For a risk-based network segmentation, the following aspects are considered:
  - Limitations for connecting IT systems to the network
  - Use of security technologies
  - Performance, trust, availability, security, and safety considerations
  - Limitation of impact in case of compromised IT systems
  - Detection of potential attacks and lateral movement of attackers
  - Separation of networks with different operational purpose (e.g. test and development networks, office network, manufacturing networks)
  - The increased risk due to network services accessible via the internet
  - Technology-specific separation options when using external IT services
  - Adequate separation between own networks and customer networks while considering customer requirements
  - Detection and prevention of data loss/leakage

Additional requirements high

- Extended requirements for the management and control of networks are determined and implemented. The following aspects are considered:
  - Authentication of IT systems on the network
  - Access to the management interfaces of IT systems is restricted
  - Specific risks (e.g. wireless and remote access)

This section deals with the management and control of your internal IT networks.

Implementation of the mandatory requirements

You determine which networks your company needs and which segmentation is required. Ideally, you should document this in writing, e. g. in a network plan or in your central *information security policy* (see Section 1.1.1).

Small companies also operate networks

This section also applies to small companies that do not appear to operate a network at first glance.

Think of a company with a small number of employees that uses workstations in a co-working space.

At least the WLAN of the operator of the co-working space is available here, sometimes a separate router is also used.

Even if the Wi-Fi is not under your control, you have still decided to use it. So, describe how the Wi-Fi is set up, whether you always use VPN connections for security reasons and similar.

If you have your own router, define the following in your router settings and document it in a network security policy, for example:

- Separation of company WLAN and guest WLAN (always useful if you want to allow guests WLAN access)
- MAC whitelisting
- Security standard used, e. g. WPA3 (currently it should be at least WPA2)
- Activation of Intrusion detection on your router
- Activation of the automatic firmware update of the router
- Change the WLAN name (this must not allow any conclusions to be drawn about the manufacturer and model of the router)
- Changing factory-assigned network keys and passwords for router administration

Implementation of the should requirements

You describe in detail further requirements for your networks and their segmentation and how you fulfil them. This must include

- How to control the connection of IT systems to networks and how to ensure that only authorized IT systems are connected.
- Which security technologies you use to protect your networks, e. g. Firewall systems or *intrusion detection* and prevention *systems* (IDS/IPS).
- What you can do to protect networks accessible from the Internet.
- Utilize separation options when separating own and customer networks (use what is technically possible and sensible).

The application of the “need-to-know” and “least privilege” principles will help you to prevent or limit data leaks and data loss. In addition, technical measures to prevent the connection of external storage media (e. g. USB sticks, external hard drives) to your computers can be useful. Alternatively, or in addition to this, automated monitoring of such connection attempts should take place.

Implementation of the additional requirements for "high" protection requirements

You also describe:

- How IT systems are authenticated in the network.
- How to restrict access to management interfaces (e. g. Intel Management Console, management interfaces, printers, WLAN, network devices).

Management interfaces

Many devices are supplied with management interfaces or interfaces activated by default. For example, printers may have an unprotected web interface that allows the download of the latest print jobs. Depending on the manufacturer, servers may have management interfaces that allow access to deeper functions (BIOS/UEFI) bypassing the operating system.

If possible, these interfaces should be deactivated, restricted or relocated to a separate network.

5.2.8 To what extent is continuity planning for IT services in place?

Quote from ISA 6.0.3

Continuity (including contingency) planning for IT services is part of an overall program for achieving continuity of operations for organizational mission and business critical functions. Actions addressed in continuity plans include orderly system degradation, system shutdown, fallback to a manual mode, alternate information flows, and operating in modes reserved for when a security incident occurs.

Must

- Critical IT services are identified, and business impact is considered.
- Requirements and responsibilities for continuity and recovery of those IT services are known to relevant stakeholders and fulfilled.

Should

- Critical IT systems are identified
  - The relevant systems are classified to have the appropriate protection need
  - Adequate and appropriate security measures are implemented

- Continuity planning includes at least the following scenarios affecting critical IT systems:
  - (Distributed) Denial of Service attacks
  - Successful ransomware attacks and other sabotage activities
  - System failure
  - Natural disaster
- Continuity planning considers the following cases
  - Alternative communication strategies, in case primary communication means are not available
  - Alternative storage strategies, in case primary storage means are not available
  - Alternative power and network
- Continuity planning is regularly reviewed and updated

Additional requirement high

- Continuity planning includes predefined time frames (Recovery Time Objective) for resumption of operation in line with requirements.
- Appropriate SLAs with external service providers according to continuity planning are in place.
- Continuity plans include coordination of contractually agreed communication with business partners
- Continuity planning is regularly tested including a full recovery and reconstitution of the system to a known state and compliance with defined target times.
- A backup and recovery strategy for critical IT services and information is defined and implemented. The following aspects are considered:
  - Backups are protected against unauthorized modification or deletion by malicious software.
  - Backups are protected against unauthorized access by malicious software or operators

Additional requirement very high

- Continuity planning is coordinated with the continuity plans of relevant external service providers.
- Continuance of essential mission and business functions with minimal or no loss of operational continuity is possible. The plan for continuance of essential mission and business functions considers the following aspects:
  - Alternate operation strategies and necessary separated standby systems to retain and/or resume operation to the extent possible if critical IT services become unavailable.
  - Alternate storage and backup sites that provide controls equivalent to that of the primary site.
- Continuity planning is tested regularly. Tests and any lessons learned are documented.

Implementation of the mandatory requirements

Your organization needs to know exactly which IT services are essential for operations and which responsibilities exist to ensure their continuous operation.

Expand the *incident handling* created in Section 1.6 to include a chapter in which you define the key services and processes that are essential for the ongoing operation of your organization.

Implementation of the should requirements

Your documentation should include possible damage scenarios for these central services that could affect your organization's ability to act and document steps for recovery or fallback options (continuity).

Your continuity planning should take into account at least the following scenarios that could affect critical IT systems: (distributed) denial of service attacks, successful ransomware attacks and other sabotage activities, system failures and natural disasters.

Continuity planning should also consider alternative communication strategies in the event of a lack of primary means of communication, alternative storage strategies for the failure of primary storage methods and alternative power supplies and networks. These scenarios can be discussed with the CERT team (see Section 1.6.2/Section 1.6.3) to determine which resources should be provided for the defined scenarios.

In addition, it is crucial that continuity planning is regularly reviewed and updated to ensure that it takes into account current threats and technological developments.

Scenario example

A typical scenario could be a successful ransomware attack on your central IT systems.

This could result in the affected systems and data being encrypted or rendered inaccessible, which would significantly impair normal operation.

Short-term continuity of your operations (e.g. availability by customers) can be ensured by means of alternative infrastructure or emergency measures (e.g. rerouting of telephones).

In parallel, alternative communication channels could be activated to maintain the flow of information within the organization if the primary means of communication are compromised. This can be done, for example, through the short-term use of encrypted messaging services on smartphones to ensure internal communication during the recovery phase.

A quick recovery can consist of using backups that are protected against alterability (e.g. in an unalterable cloud archive or in a physically separate storage system) to restore all systems.

Schedule a regular review (at least annually) of the scenarios, services and resources described in the *action plan.*

Implementation of additional requirements for "high" protection requirements

Expand the description of incident handling scenarios to include clear recovery time objectives (RTOs) that correspond to business requirements, i.e. derived from any contractual requirements or your own objectives.

External services or systems may be covered by service level agreements (SLAs), and these should be checked against the RTO targets set and adjusted if necessary.

Requirements of this standard chapter for the backup and restore strategy are covered by Section 5.2.9.

Implementation of additional requirements for "very high" protection requirements

You should ensure that the continuity requirements are compatible with the agreements with the relevant external service providers, so that scenarios that affect the services of central suppliers should be coordinated with them to ensure that the planned continuity measures can be taken. For example, if you are planning to reroute your communication in an emergency, this should also be realizable at short notice with the selected service provider.

To fulfil the requirements in the "very high" category, you should ensure that the most central services receive special attention during planning. Check whether further measures can be taken to enable your core services and processes to run smoothly.

To ensure the operational continuity of a web shop or ERP, for example, hosters that enable geo-redundancy of the system could be considered in order to prevent the failure of a single data center.

Ensure that the regular review of the scenarios (described under "should") involves stakeholders (e. g. CERT) and that results and potential for improvement are documented (e. g. directly in the action plan).

5.2.9 To what extent is the backup and recovery of data and IT services guaranteed?

Quote from ISA 6.0.3

Data and IT services can become unavailable through events such as hardware failures, software defects, operator errors or attacks. Backup and recovery enables organizations to recover from relevant situations and limit potential harm to the organization to a reasonable amount.

Must

- Backup concepts exist for relevant IT systems. The following aspects are considered:
  - Appropriate protective measures to ensure confidentiality, integrity, and availability for data backups
- Recovery concepts exist for relevant IT services.

Should

- A backup and recovery concept exists for each relevant IT service.
  - Dependencies between IT services and the sequence for recovery are considered

Additional requirement high

- Backup and recovery concepts are methodically reviewed at regular intervals.
- Generals restore capability is considered and tested (e.g., sample testing, test systems)
- Backup and recovery concepts consider the following aspects:
  - Recovery Point Objective (RPO)
  - Recovery Time Objective (RTO)
  - Required resources for recovery (considering capacity and performance incl. personnel and hardware)
  - Avoidance of overload scenarios during recovery
  - Appropriate spatial redundancy (e.g., separate room, separate firesection, separate datacentre, separate site)

Additional requirement very high

- (Additional) Backups are performed via offline procedures, immutable backups or by using isolated IAM technology.
- Restore procedures are technically tested in a methodical way at regular intervals.
- Geographical redundancy is considered in data backup and recovery concepts.

Implementation of the mandatory requirements

A backup concept should be created that covers all relevant IT systems.

Create a *backup policy* that describes your basic procedure for creating and restoring data backups. In the backup policy, also list which systems are backed up, using which method, how often and to where.

Implementation of the should requirements

Check the backup policy with regard to the completeness of the listed systems, so that all relevant IT systems are taken into account.

> **Backup by third parties**
>
> If systems are partly backed up by service providers and service contracts, it is also advisable to list these in the backup policy with a corresponding note in order to provide a complete overview.

You should check whether there are specific dependencies that require a certain sequence when restoring services. If this is the case, these should also be taken into account accordingly in the description of any restore procedures in the backup policy.

Implementation of additional requirements for "high" protection requirements

Schedule a regular (quarterly) review of the backup topic in the *action plan*. You should take the following aspects into account in this planning:

- General overview of the status of the systems, including expected utilized storage capacities, necessary resources for new systems
- Checking any faulty backups and logs
- Checking the security of newly introduced systems

In the list of the backup policy, describe the requirements per system with regard to restore point and restore time (RTO/RPO). In case of doubt, these requirements can also be determined via a risk assessment in order to find a balance between effort and possible risk (e. g. due to a lengthy recovery).

Make sure that backups are regularly stored in at least two, preferably three different locations. For example, you could mirror backups to another physical location and also store them in encrypted form in a cloud service.

Implementation of additional requirements for "very high" protection requirements

If a very high level of protection is required, the backups should be additionally protected:

Consider protecting your backups against changes such as ransomware by storing some of them offline or unchangeable (read-only memory, cloud archives). Alternatively, the backups can also be protected by an authentication mechanism that is decoupled from the productive systems (no SSO or etc.) in order to come as close as possible to immutability.

In addition to quarterly spot checks of backups, explicit recovery tests should also be carried out to ensure that data backups are fundamentally integer, the defined process is functional and planned RTO&RPO can be achieved.

5.3 System acquisition, requirements management and development

5.3.1 To what extent is information security considered in new or further developed IT systems?

Quote from ISA 6.0.3

Information security is an integral part of the entire lifecycle of IT systems. This particularly includes consideration of information security requirements in the development or acquisition of IT systems.

Must

- The information security requirements associated with the design and development of IT systems are determined and considered.
- The information security requirements associated with the acquisition or extension of IT systems and IT components are determined and considered.
- Information security requirements associated with changes to developed IT systems are considered.
- System approval tests are carried out under consideration of the information security requirements.

Should

- Requirement specifications are prepared. The following aspects are considered:
  - The information security requirements
  - Vendor recommendations and best practices for secure configuration and implementation
  - Best practices and security guidelines
  - Fail safe (designed to return to a safe condition in the event of a failure or malfunction)
- Requirement specifications are reviewed against the information security requirements.
- The IT system is reviewed for compliance with specifications prior to productive use.
  - The use of productive data for testing purposes is avoided as far as possible (if applicable, anonymization or pseudonymization)
  - Where productive data are used for testing purposes, it shall be ensured that the test system is provided with protective measures comparable to those on the operational system

  - Requirements for the lifecycle of test data (e.g. deletion, maximum lifetime on the IT system)
  - Case-related specifications for the generation of test data are defined

Additional requirements very high

- The security of purpose-built software or significantly customized software is tested (e.g. penetration testing)
  - During commissioning
  - In case of significant changes
  - Or at regular intervals

This section aims to ensure that security requirements are already taken into account in the design and development of new systems.

Implementation of the mandatory requirements

Requirements

Create a *change management* document that basically describes how information security is taken into account in the planning and development of IT systems. Describe:

- How can changes to systems be requested from your company's IT department?
- How are changes prioritized and classified? Ideally, changes are categorized into three classes according to their impact on information security (normal impact, high impact, very high impact).
- Depending on the classes, the ISO should be involved in the definition, implementation and acceptance of changes with a high impact.

Documentation Dealing with changes (example)

- Change ID
- Planned change
- Affected systems
- Information security requirements
- Technical details
- Influence on information security
- Authorized
- Risk of change
- Test the change
- Result of the test
- Corrective action
- Responsible
- Communication
- Status

Procurement

In addition, requirements for the procurement of components and systems should be defined. Describe the minimum requirements for commonly procured components, systems and solutions in your company in an *IT procurement guideline* document:

- Minimum requirements for computers and servers: Aspects such as Trusted Platform modules, support for encryption or network security standards.
- Minimum requirements for systems: Use of current software technologies, support of certain security features for authentication or support of current operating systems.
- Minimum requirement for services or cloud services: Support for integration via single sign-on (SSO; login that is valid for different systems at the same time), end-to-end encryption.

Implementation of the should requirements

Specifications

Specify in the *IT procurement guideline* that systems with a high degree of complexity are selected on the basis of a specification sheet or catalogue of requirements to be drawn up. The ISO must be consulted during the creation process.

The requirements in the specifications should be reviewed again before the systems are put into operation and should include aspects relating to the implementation of security measures (e. g. requirements for encryption, integration into local authentication mechanisms), configuration options, implementation of best practices and requirements for fail-safe/restore options.

If possible, carry out tests in advance. For example, the IT department can test software in test mode against the requirements and check all configurations before the system is set up and connected to the production network.

Test data

If possible, avoid using production data for system tests. If you still have to use production data for tests, you should define suitable protective measures (similar security level as in production operation, requirements for the life cycle of the production data in the test system (focus on deletion) and case-related requirements depending on the classification) or anonymize the data beforehand or cleanse it of information worthy of protection.

The creation of test data on the basis of productive data should only take place on the basis of a release by IT or ISO. Ideally, you should create a list of the test data records created to ensure that they are deleted at the end of the project/project.

Describe your regulations for the use of test data in the *Change Management* document.

Implementation of additional requirements for "very high" protection requirements

If your organization uses custom-developed software, a penetration test or system audit should be carried out regularly. This should be implemented analogue to the requirements in Section 5.2.6 by including these systems in the planning for auditing IT systems.

5.3.2 To what extent are requirements for network services defined?

Quote from ISA 6.0.3

Network services have different requirements for information security, quality of data transfer or management. It is important to know these criteria and the scope of use of the different network services.

Must

- Requirements regarding the information security of network services are determined and fulfilled.

Should

- A procedure for securing and using network services is defined and implemented.
- The requirements are agreed in the form of SLAs.
- Adequate redundancy solutions are implemented.

Additional requirements high

- Procedures for monitoring the quality of network traffic (e. g. traffic flow analyses, availability measurements) are defined and carried out.

Implementation of the mandatory requirements

Determine and fulfil requirements

It is advisable to document all requirements for the configuration and operation of networks in a centralized *network security policy* in close coordination with the IT department.

The following aspects should be regulated and documented:

- An overview of the networks operated in the company (ideally linking to a network diagram)
- An overview of the protective measures taken (e. g. Network disconnection, IDS, IPS, firewall, RADIUS, etc.).
- An overview of outsourced networks/networks provided by service providers (e. g. Telephony, rented network resources in the data center)

Implementation of the should requirements

Securing and using network services

The protective measures defined in the *network security policy* should be checked for appropriateness for each network in close cooperation with IT. The measures taken should be checked for appropriateness in the risk assessment.

Furthermore, measures must be documented that guarantee the security of information transmission as far as possible when connecting to external networks. This includes, for example, the documentation of security measures when sending e-mails or VoIP connections.

If you use third-party network services (e. g. maintenance of internal networks by service providers, rented capacity in data centers), the security and availability requirements must be agreed in the form of SLAs. The concluded SLAs should be referenced in the *network security policy*.

Redundancy solutions

The use of redundancy solutions (e. g. back-up lines, backup capacities, hot standby of servers) may be necessary to meet your availability requirements.

The need to create such redundancy capacities should be examined by means of a risk assessment. A second Internet line, for example, is also conceivable for small companies in order to bridge outages.

If you identify the need for a redundancy solution as part of the risk assessment or your customer has specific requirements for the availability of services, these measures should be implemented until the test is completed.

You also document the implemented measures in the *network security policy*, depending on the individual networks.

Implementation of additional requirements for "high" protection requirements

Network traffic should be monitored where possible in order to analyze capacity bottlenecks or availability times.

As a rule, simple analyses are already possible in the management consoles of network hardware or the firewall. It is also possible to integrate these devices into monitoring systems in order to actively and automatically monitor certain measured assets.

Aspects are for example:

- Availability and downtimes of networks and Internet connections
- Bandwidths used in local networks as well as Internet connections (e. g. Speed test in smaller networks)

- Active network services and accumulated data volumes
- Runtimes of typical requests (DHCP, DNS)
- Security-related metrics (e. g. number of blocked connections) also in SaaS such as Microsoft 365

You can document the monitoring parameters defined for each network in the *network security policy*.

5.3.3 To what extent is the return and secure removal of information assets from external IT services regulated?

Quote from ISA 6.0.3

In order to ensure control over the information assets as the information owner, it is necessary that the information assets can be safely removed or are returned, if required, when terminating the IT service.

Must

- A procedure for the return and secure removal of information assets from each external IT service is defined and implemented.

Should

- A description of the termination process is given, adapted to any changes, and contractually regulated.

Implementation of the mandatory requirements

Return procedure

For each service provider listed in the *IT cloud provider directory*, a procedure should be defined to ensure the complete removal of your information assets in the event of contract termination.

To do this, expand the *IT cloud provider directory* to include a checklist that takes into account aspects of the end of the contract for each service used. The following aspects could play an important role here:

- Will you receive a notification if the service is cancelled by the provider?
- Will your data be handed over to you in a usable format at the end of the contract?
- Is the procedure, any costs and the period for returning or handing over your data at the end of the contract defined?
- Do you have the right to access the metadata generated by the cloud service system at the end of the contract?

- Are your data and the associated metadata immediately and permanently destroyed at the end of the contract in such a way that it cannot be reconstructed?
- Does the company send confirmation of the deletion of the data and metadata to the provider before the services are terminated?
- Is there a way for the company to terminate the service contract without penalties if the provider changes its cloud service?

Use this checklist when scheduling so that all of the above aspects are taken into account and ensured.

Implementation of the should requirements

Provider responsibility

These questions defined under the mandatory requirements of this section should be answered with reference to the contract documents to ensure that a clean and regulated termination is possible and that the provider assures responsibility for the respective provider-side points (e. g. provision of a data export).

As part of the *action plan*, define an annual review of this checklist to ensure that these issues continue to apply.

5.3.4 To what extent is information protected in shared external IT services?

Quote from ISA 6.0.3

Clear segregation between individual clients must be ensured such as to always protect own information in external IT services and to prevent it from being accessed by other organizations (clients).

Must

- Effective segregation (e. g. segregation of clients) prevents access to own information by unauthorized users of other organizations.

Should

- The provider's segregation concept is documented and adapted to any changes. The following aspects are considered:
  - Separation of data, functions, customer-specific software, operating system, storage system and network
  - Risk assessment for the operation of external software within the shared environment

Implementation of the mandatory requirements

Client separation

Check the concepts and technical descriptions of all providers listed in the *IT cloud provider directory*.

For each provider, you should summarize and document whether client separation is guaranteed. In each case, refer to the proof or part of the contract in which the provider promises client separation.

Implementation of the should requirements

Documentation

Ideally, a separation concept should be available for each provider. Check whether your provider provides technical documentation describing the separation concept that addresses common technical aspects (e. g. Separation at data level, network separation, use of encryption). You should check this technical documentation again for appropriateness and reference it in *the IT cloud provider directory*. If possible, further hardening measures should be implemented by configuration on your part.

If third-party software is used in a shared environment, create a *risk assessment* to check this.

6 Supplier Relationships

6.1 Supplier relationships

This chapter deals with the cooperation with the contractors you have commissioned and with cooperation partners. This also includes all of your legally independent subsidiaries or partner companies.

You assess potential risks arising from these collaborations for information security. You will also conclude non-disclosure agreements (NDA) if required.

6.1.1 To what extent is information security ensured for contractors and cooperation partners?

Quote from ISA 6.0.3

An appropriate level of information security is also maintained while collaborating with cooperation partners and contractors.

Must

- Contractors and cooperation partners are subjected to a risk assessment with regard to information security.
- An appropriate level of information security is ensured by contractual agreements with contractors and cooperation partners.
- Where applicable, contractual agreements with clients are passed on to contractors and cooperation partners.
- Compliance with contractual agreements is verified.

Should

- Contractors and cooperation partners are contractually obliged to pass on any requirements regarding an appropriate level of information security to their subcontractors.
- Service reports and documents by contractors and cooperation partners are reviewed.

Additional requirements high

- Proof is provided that the information security level of the supplier is adequate for the protection needs of the information (e. g. certificate, attestation, internal audit).

Implementation of the mandatory requirements

You carry out an evaluation of all suppliers currently commissioned or commissioned in the near future (supplier assessment) and document the results in writing. You also evaluate any new suppliers that are added later in time. The evaluation must be repeated regularly – at least once a year.

If you already have a quality management system (QMS), you will be familiar with the supplier evaluation process. You can either expand the existing supplier evaluation procedure from the QMS to include the requirements of information security or introduce a separate supplier evaluation procedure for information security.

Please note: Supplier evaluation for the purposes of information security differs from supplier evaluation in terms of quality. It is therefore not about things like prices and delivery reliability, but about possible risk factors for information security.

The first step is to identify all of your company's suppliers, if you have not already done so. In a second step, you determine which of your suppliers have an impact on your company's information security. In most companies, only a small proportion of existing suppliers have an impact on information security.

Further steps now follow, focusing on the suppliers with an influence on information security: Among other things, you assess whether, in your view, the contractual agreements are sufficient with regard to maintaining confidentiality in business transactions.

Whenever you come to a negative result here, the contracts must be renewed or extended in order to achieve a sufficient level of security.

You document the results of your evaluation, including the approval or non-approval of suppliers, in your supplier evaluation table or in your existing CRM system. A three-stage evaluation scheme is suitable for this (Table 6.1).

Table 6.1 Three-stage evaluation scheme

Risk class of the supplier	Criteria for categorization in a risk class
low	The Supplier or its subcontractors shall not have access to confidential or highly confidential information or to the Company's premises.
medium	The Supplier or its subcontractors shall have access to confidential or strictly confidential information or to the Company's premises. The Supplier is at the same time bound to confidentiality by contractual agreements with the Company or by applicable professional law. If the Supplier engages subcontractors, they shall be bound to confidentiality if they are given access to confidential or strictly confidential information or to Company premises.
high	The Supplier or its subcontractors shall have access to confidential or strictly confidential information or to Company premises. The Supplier shall not be bound to confidentiality by contractual agreements with the Company or by applicable law. If the Supplier engages subcontractors, they shall not be bound to confidentiality if they are given access to confidential or strictly confidential information or to Company premises.

You should accept at maximum suppliers in the "medium" risk class. If a supplier falls into the "high" risk category after the first assessment, risk minimization measures must be implemented and a new assessment carried out on this basis. These measures may include (selection)

- Rectification of the contract
- Determination of additional agreement or contractual penalties
- Carrying out supplier audits to check critical areas and compliance with established rules
- Provision of certificates as proof of an information security management system

Whenever you want to commission new suppliers, you must carry out a supplier evaluation in accordance with the requirements described before placing a binding order. It would be wrong to commission the supplier first and only evaluate them with a time delay in the next regular supplier evaluation cycle!

To ensure the timely evaluation of new suppliers, you need a process that you document in a purchasing guideline or a supplier guideline. If necessary, train the employees involved in this new process.

If you yourself commission subcontractors or partners to process customer orders, inform all these subcontractors or partners about the requirements of your client (as far as information security is concerned).

You are also obliged to regularly check compliance with the contractual requirements. This applies to the requirements that are placed on you, but also the requirements that you place on subcontractors and partners. To this end, you must carry out a self-assessment at least once a year and document the results.

Implementation of the should requirements

Determine which of your contractors and cooperation partners use subcontractors. Also consider IT companies that may have outsourced parts of their development to freelancers abroad, or cleaning or security services, as they often use subcontractors.

If the existing contracts with these contractors and cooperation partners do not contain sufficient provisions on subcontractors, it is advisable to draw up a supplementary agreement or a non-disclosure agreement. This should state that the contractor or cooperation partner is obliged to maintain the confidentiality of all its subcontractors.

If they are subcontractors who are given access to your premises, instead of adding an addendum to the contract, you can simply have every visitor who comes from an external company sign a confidentiality agreement every time they enter your premises.

You also continuously check all service reports and logs sent to you by your contractors and co-operation partners.

Implementation of additional requirements for "high" protection requirements

If you have certificates or similar evidence that prove the supplier has a certain level of information security, keep them. It is a good idea to document these documents – or references to them – either in the supplier's master data or in your supplier evaluation. In the case of certificates with a limited validity period – e. g. certificates for management systems – the expiry date of the certificate should also be documented here.

Examples of the documents required here: Certificate of an existing ISMS in accordance with ISO 27001 from a supplier. Report of a supplier's self-disclosure on information security issues.

6.1.2 To what extent is non-disclosure regarding the exchange of information contractually agreed?

Quote from ISA 6.0.3

Non-disclosure agreements provide legal protection of an organization's information particularly where information is exchanged beyond the boundaries of the organization.

Must

- The non-disclosure requirements are determined and fulfilled.
- Requirements and procedures for applying non-disclosure agreements are known to all persons passing on information in need of protection.

- Valid non-disclosure agreements are concluded prior to forwarding sensitive information.
- The requirements and procedures for the use of non-disclosure agreements and the handling of information requiring protection are reviewed at regular intervals.

Should

- Non-disclosure agreement templates are available and checked for legal applicability
- Non-disclosure agreements include the following information:
  - The persons/organizations involved
  - The type of information covered by the agreement
  - The subject of the agreement
  - The validity period of the agreement
  - The responsibilities of the obliged party
- Non-disclosure agreements include provisions for the handling of sensitive information beyond the contractual relationship.
- Options of demonstrating compliance with specifications (e.g. review by an independent third party or audit rights) are defined.
- A process for monitoring the validity period of temporary non-disclosure agreements and initiating their extension in due time is defined and implemented.

Implementation of the mandatory requirements

As part of the supplier evaluation (Section 6.1.1), also check whether sufficient non-disclosure agreements are in place.

You create a sample non-disclosure agreement that you can have other parties sign if required. You do this for all current and future business partners.

You also define how confidentiality agreements are to be handled internally. In particular, you must regulate when they are to be used, who is responsible for obtaining signatures and where the agreements are to be stored.

The template for your supplier assessment is a controlled document and as such must have a version number and be approved by an authorized person within the company. You should therefore also specify the storage location of the template and inform the employees concerned. This will minimize the risk of outdated versions of the template being used by your employees.

Compliance with these rules must be checked, e.g. as part of your annual internal audits (see Section 1.5.1).

Implementation of the should requirements

You include all the minimum contents specified in Section 6.1.2 of the standard in your model non-disclosure agreement.

Ideally, you should obtain audit rights from the contractual partner, although this will not always be possible. Alternatively, it is a good idea to ask the partner to provide evidence of information security certifications, if any exist.

Wherever possible, the validity of the confidentiality agreement should extend beyond the contractual relationship in order to protect confidential information even after the cooperation has ended.

Have your sample non-disclosure agreement checked by a competent person (ideally a lawyer).

If there are temporary non-disclosure agreements, monitor their deadlines so that you can arrange for them to be extended in good time. You can delegate this to your legal department or purchasing department, for example. The procedure for monitoring these temporary non-disclosure agreements must also be reviewed. This can again be done as part of internal audits (see Section 1.5.1).

Close confidentiality obligations early!

Confidentiality agreements should always be concluded *before* any data is exchanged, even if no order has yet been placed!

In practice, this applies to anyone to whom you provide deeper insight into your company in any form, e. g. also consultants or potential buyers of your company if you are planning a sale.

If you grant suppliers or other parties access to your systems – such as a folder with internal company documents in your cloud storage – you should document the access granted. The supplier evaluation table is ideal for this. This allows you to keep track of the access granted and deactivate it again if necessary.

7 Compliance

7.1 Aligning the company with laws and guidelines

The chapter aims to incorporate and take into account the legal requirements and the context of the organization in the ISMS.

7.1.1 To what extent is compliance with regulatory and contractual provisions ensured?

Quote from ISA 6.0.3

Non-compliance with legal, regulatory, or contractual provisions can create risks to the information security of customers and the own organization. Therefore, it is essential to ensure that these provisions are known and observed.

Must

- Legal, regulatory, and contractual provisions of relevance to information security (see examples) are determined at regular intervals.
- Policies regarding compliance with the provisions are defined, implemented, and communicated to the responsible persons.

Should

- The integrity of records in accordance with the legal, regulatory, or contractual provisions and business requirements is considered.

The aim is to ensure that external requirements (laws, regulations and contractual requirements) are taken into account when designing the ISMS.

Implementation of the mandatory requirements

Determination of requirements

The requirements must be determined and ideally documented. It is advisable to implement the following documents for this purpose:

Procedure for identifying requirements: This process description should record who determines requirements for the ISMS and derives the necessary measures from this.

Process description of requirements (example)

The Information Security Officer (ISO) is responsible for recording all requirements for the company with regard to information security. This includes legal, contractual, self-imposed and regulatory requirements. This also includes the registration of interested parties.

The requirements can be recorded together with the specialist managers.

The ISO is responsible for identifying the people in the company who have an influence on such requirements.

The ISO is responsible for documenting all requirements and agreeing the list with the management as part of the management review.

Document all requirements arising from specific business relationships, such as reporting information security incidents, handling prototypes, etc.

It is advisable to transfer this responsibility to the ISO as a matter of principle – close cooperation should take place with specialized departments (data protection officer for data protection laws, accounting for commercial issues, purchasing for contract requirements).

All requirements documented in this section should be reviewed annually. Ideally, you should schedule the review of the following documents in the *action plan*.

Interested parties: The interested parties (stakeholders) in relation to the organization should be documented here. Interested parties may have a direct or indirect influence on information security and may be in a conflicting relationship. The following aspects should be documented:

- Interested party
- Summary of expectations of your company and your security
- Assessment of the impact on the success of your security measures and ISMS
- Last update

Exemplary entries are:

- **Customers:** Have high expectations of information security and compliance, but at the same time want fast and unbureaucratic cooperation. Generally, have a high level of influence on your ISMS and the security objectives set (e. g. through the requirement to implement this standard).

- **Employees:** Wish for easy-to-implement security rules and trust. Expect data to be treated confidentially. Generally, have a high influence on the success of the ISMS, as the success of the implementation of security measures depends on the willingness of the workforce to cooperate.
- **Competitors:** Depending on the context, competitors may be interested in your failure or in creating a bad image. They could do this, for example, by disclosing or publicizing your security deficiencies. There is at least a small indirect influence on your ISMS. Depending on the context, your competitors may also be unscrupulous and not shy away from active measures (espionage, manipulation, hacking).
- **Public:** Depending on the context, the public may also be interested in your level of security or compliance with legal regulations (e. g. if you are a service provider for the banking sector). A medium to high influence is conceivable, for example, if a negative public opinion also has a negative impact on your customer relationships.

Legal cadaster: All laws applicable to the company should be documented in this document. In addition, the following must be documented:

- Which business area is affected by this?
- Who is responsible for implementation (compliance)?
- What steps will be taken if the laws are changed?
- When was the law last reviewed?

Focus on ISMS

In order to fulfil the standard, it is particularly relevant that you document laws that are directly related to the ISMS. This also includes peripheral issues such as compliance with retention periods in accounting: Technical security measures have a direct influence on the implementation of such legal requirements.

However, it can also be helpful to document all laws relevant to the company. The *legal cadaster* then takes on a universal character beyond the ISMS. This applies to all documents in Section 7.1.1 anyway – ideally, you should coordinate these documents closely with the management.

Table 7.1 shows some examples of applicable laws for Germany, depending on your country laws regarding to retention and storage of data, security compliance and data protection may apply to you.

For example, HIPAA in the USA governs the protection of health-related data, while laws such as the CCPA regulate consumer data privacy. Similarly, employee protection regulations like the FMLA or Title VII of the Civil Rights Act may impose specific requirements concerning the handling of employee data and workplace compliance.

Table 7.1 Relevant laws

Range	Title	Summary
Data protection	**GDPR and BDSG**	Compliance with data protection principles, reporting obligations, DSM
	TDDDG	Compliance with data protection for online services
Information security	**GeschGehG**	Protection of trade secrets
	StGB § 202a, 202b, 202c, 206, 263a, 268–274, 303a, 303b, 317	Offences in the area of computer sabotage, espionage
	ITSiG IT Security Act	(applies to energy suppliers, for example)
	Security Review Act	(e. g. relevant for authorities, public bodies)
	TKÜV	(applies to certain service providers, for example)
	TMG	(applies to certain service providers, for example)
Employment relationship	**UrhG § 69a, 106**	Regulations on the applicability of copyright law
	BetrVG	Effects on employee data protection
	SGB I § 35	Handling of social data
	SGB X § 67–78	
	TKG (§ 3(5), § 88)	Obligations as a telecommunications provider, telecommunications secrecy
	Administrative Procedure Act § 30	(may apply to public organizations)
Accounting	**HGB § 37a, § 257**	Compliance with retention and record-keeping obligations
	AO § 145–147	
	AktG Section 91 (2)	Obligations to keep proper records, operation of monitoring system
	GmbHG § 41 para. 1	Obligations for the proper keeping of books
	HGB	Principles of proper accounting
	GoB	
	GoBD	Principles of proper accounting and storage in electronic form
	KonTraG	Obligations to maintain an early warning system

Further requirements: This is where you document requirements that cannot be derived directly from a law, but which nevertheless have a direct influence on the design of your ISMS.

This should also be documented in each case:

- Summary of the requirement
- Business areas affected
- Actions to be initiated in the event of a change
- Last check

Other requirements include

- The standard that you implement at the customer's request
- Requirements for reporting information security incidents to customers (this can also be part of contracts at the customer's request and should be explicitly mentioned here)
- Special information security requirements from individual customer contracts

You should also document key sources of information that you use to obtain relevant industry developments or security incident reports. For example:

- CVE reports
- Vulnerability Newsletter
- Industry associations from which you obtain information

Implementation of the should requirements

Fulfilment of intellectual property rights

Licence requirements must be taken into account when procuring software. The licence models of today's software, especially cloud services, make it more difficult to actively violate these licence models.

Nevertheless, it is advisable to regularly check whether all users are correctly licensed. To do this, plan an annual review of all software licenses in the *action plan*: For example, compare software licenses that can be viewed in administration portals with the number of users created.

If you develop software within the company, it is recommended that you also check the license conditions of integrated frameworks and third-party software in this context in order to rule out a license violation.

Awareness

The annual employee training courses should take compliance into account. Specifically, you should convey the following aspects to employees:

- Legal requirements to be complied with for the respective work area
- Copyright compliance depending on the area of work (e. g. media data for the marketing department, software licensing for IT and developers)
- Raising awareness of compliance with information security regulations as an important part of the company's compliance – also in terms of customer requirements

Integrity of records

If there are requirements for the integrity of records (prescribed retention period of logs, protocols) in contracts or (industry-specific) laws that affect you, these requirements must be documented in the documents from Section 7.1.1 (*legal cadaster* and *other requirements*).

The implementation must then be taken into account in the respective documents, e. g. the *logging policy*.

7.1.2 To what extent is the protection of personally identifiable data considered when implementing information security?

Quote from ISA 6.0.3

Privacy and protection of personally identifiable data are considered in the implementation of information security as required by relevant national legislation and regulations, where applicable.

Must

- Legal and contractual information security requirements regarding the procedures and processes in the processing of personally identifiable data are determined.
- Regulations regarding the compliance with legal and contractual requirements for the protection of personally identifiable data are defined and known to the entrusted persons.
- Processes and procedures for the protection of personally identifiable data are considered in the information security management system.

Information security and data protection are particularly interdependent. This is why the Information Security module includes data protection as an explicit chapter.

Appointment of a data protection officer

Due to your activity or company size, you may not even be covered by the designation obligation of the European GDPR. Nevertheless, it is advisable to appoint a person to implement the statutory data protection provisions in Europe to clearly map responsibilities, reporting channels and dependencies on the ISMS. Similar may apply to you outside of Europe if you handle Personal Identifiable Information (PII) for OEMs.

If you are outside of the scope of the GDPR, measurement that would affect only your employees PII and not PII handled for the OEM like video surveillance on your property are probably out of scope.

Implementation of the mandatory requirements

In order to provide proof of implementation of the mandatory requirements, you should coordinate the following documentation closely with your data protection officer and check that it is up to date:

- The data protection officer should have up-to-date proof of expertise (e. g. participation in a training course).
- The data protection officer should be included in the organization chart.
- The documentation of the processing operations should be up to date (including legal basis, storage location, impact assessment, where applicable, storage duration).
- The privacy policy should be up to date.
- Video surveillance should be included in the documentation (processing operations, privacy policy).
- Signets and signs for video surveillance should be available. Ideally, photographs of these can be submitted as evidence in the audit.
- A current activity report of the data protection officer should be available.
- A data protection manual for central processes (deletion concept, fulfilment of data subject rights) should be available.
- The procedure for the timely erasure of data in accordance with the erasure concept and the storage period documented in the processing directory should be verifiable (e. g. via documentation in the action plan, configured automatic erasure in systems).

Consideration of customer and employee data

Also check whether the privacy policy and documented processing operations relate only to the website or also correctly to customer and employee data (e.g. Newsletter, CRM, time recording).

8 Prototype Protection

Quote from ISA 6.0.3

Prototype protection protects physical prototypes which are classified as requiring protection. Prototypes include vehicles, components, and parts. The owner of the intellectual property for the prototype is considered the owner of the prototype.

The owner's commissioning department is responsible for classifying the protection need of a prototype. For prototypes classified as requiring high or very high protection, the minimum requirements for prototype protection must be applied.

8.1 Physical and environmental security

Quote from ISA 6.0.3

The requirements described in this section apply to all companies which, on their own properties, manufacture, store or are provided for use vehicles, components or parts classified as requiring protection.

The section aims to ensure security against theft and insight at the company sites where prototypes (vehicles) are parked, stored or processed.

The standard first provides the following definition of prototype protection: "Prototype protection protects physical prototypes that are categorized as requiring protection. Prototypes include vehicles, components and parts. The owner of the intellectual property for the prototype is considered the owner of the prototype.

The owner's commissioning department is responsible for categorizing the protection requirements of a prototype. For prototypes that are classified as prototypes with a high or very high protection requirement, the minimum requirements for prototype protection must be applied."

In practice, your customers decide what is to be considered a prototype. Usually, drawings or images of prototypes are not classified as prototypes themselves.

8.1.1 To what extent is a security concept available describing minimum requirements regarding the physical and environmental security for prototype protection?

Quote from ISA 6.0.3

The necessary measures for prototype protection must be applied to and implemented on properties and facilities of suppliers, development partners and service providers. A security concept must be established by the respective operator. Implementation and observation of the physical and environmental security measures defined in the security concept must be ensured by the responsible operator.

Must

- A security concept under consideration of the following aspects is established:
  - Stability of outer skin
  - View and sight protection
  - Protection against unauthorized entry and access control
  - Intrusion monitoring
  - Documented visitor management
  - Client segregation

Should

- Perimeter security.

Implementation of the mandatory requirements

You can and should use the security zone concept as defined in your access policy (see Section 3.1.1). Do not create a separate security zone concept but expand the existing one. Make this extension for all your locations where you store prototype parts or prototype vehicles.

The following aspects are new and need to be assessed:

- *Security of the outer shell:* Firstly, check that the outer skin of your property is secure. If the outer skin of your property is not made of concrete or brickwork, you should carry out a more detailed check. Does the outer skin still offer burglary protection against thieves using standard tools such as hammers or crowbars? Can it be broken through with a (possibly stolen prototype vehicle)? Especially if the outer skin is made of drywall or wooden walls, security is jeopardized.

- *Visibility and view protection:* Check whether the windows offer sufficient privacy protection against views from neighboring properties or from guests on your company property. Even when doors, windows and roller shutters are open, it must not be possible to see prototype vehicles or prototype parts. Also consider the visual and viewing protection within (!) your property. Adequate protection must also be provided against viewing by e. g. non-project employees or visitors.
- *Protection against unauthorized entry and access control:* Re-evaluate the measures you have already defined. Do they provide sufficient protection for the prototype parts and prototype vehicles you store?
- *Burglary surveillance:* Are the existing burglar alarms, cameras and/or patrols sufficient?
- *Documented visitor management:* Check whether your existing visitor management is sufficient, especially with regard to client separation, see the next point.
- *Client separation:* Ensure that only authorized persons have access to and insight into prototype parts and prototype vehicles. This also includes listening of confidential conversations relating to prototypes. Clients, in this context, include employees as well as visitors, service providers and representatives of OEMs.

At this point, TISAX does not provide detailed specifications on how the requirements should be implemented. Due to the very different situations in each company, only individual solutions can be found.

It is therefore important that you first carry out a thorough and unvarnished inventory. Any gaps and weaknesses that you identify must then be eliminated or sufficiently minimized through measures that you define. You document the state you are aiming for in your security zone concept. Be prepared for the TISAX auditor to ask questions about this and demand a plausible explanation.

It is not enough to describe the security zone concept. The measures defined there must be demonstrably implemented. For this purpose, an on-site assessment is carried out by the TISAX assessor for all requirements from Chapter 8.

If you have several locations and no prototype parts are stored at individual locations – e. g. at an office-only location – these locations do not have to fulfil the requirements of Chapter 8. It is important to document this clearly in your security zone concept.

Please also note: The entire Section 8.1 deals with security at immobile locations. The transport of prototypes and the handling of them at temporary locations – e. g. during test drives – are not affected by Section 8.1.

Implementation of the should requirements

In addition to the "must" requirements, the perimeter protection (e. g. fences or walls that make access to your property difficult) is also required. Proceed as described here. The perimeter security should make it more difficult for burglars to enter your property. If you store prototype vehicles on your premises, you should prevent or make it impossible for potential thieves to leave the company premises with these vehicles.

8.1.2 To what extent is perimeter security existent preventing unauthorized access to protected property objects?

Quote from ISA 6.0.3

Unauthorized access to properties where vehicles, components or parts classified as requiring protection are manufactured, processed, or stored shall be prevented.

Must

- Unauthorized access to properties is not possible.

Should

- Suitable barriers are in place such as:
  - Artificial barriers (fence systems, walls)
  - Technical barriers (detection)
  - Natural barriers (growth, vegetation)

Implementation of the mandatory requirements

Here you build directly on what you have developed in Section 8.1.1. You have already added perimeter protection requirements to your security zone concept there.

In more detail, ask yourself whether the existing perimeter security offers sufficient protection against unauthorized access to your property premises. This applies in particular to the common types of intrusion: climbing over, undermining and cutting through.

It should therefore be checked, for example, whether an existing wire fence offers sufficient protection against climbing over. How high is it? Is it secured with barbed wire? As wire fences usually have no foundation, you should check how easy it is for burglars to undermine the wire fence and thus gain access to your property. Is the ground hard or soft? Is there any unevenness in the ground, so that there are already gaps between the bottom of the wire fence and the ground in some places? The stability of the wire fence itself should also be checked: How easily can it be cut – e. g. using a bolt cutter?

Implementation of the should requirements

You ensure that your properties have adequate perimeter protection for the entire site and document this in your security zone concept.

Perimeter security also includes protective measures such as motion detectors and alarm systems. Natural barriers such as vegetation or earth walls, if present, should also be taken into account.

If your location does not have a factory site, you should still set this standard chapter to applicable and assign yourself a maturity level. If your site has a sufficiently secure outer shell, you can classify this as perimeter security. With sufficient documentation, a maturity level 3 in the self-assessment may be justified here.

8.1.3 To what extent is the outer skin of the protected buildings constructing such as to prevent removal or opening of outer-skin components using standard tools?

Quote from ISA 6.0.3

Unauthorized access to buildings/security areas where vehicles, components or parts classified as requiring protection are manufactured, processed or stored shall be prevented.

Must

- Unauthorized access to buildings/security areas is not possible.

Should

- Solid construction (masonry, concrete, reinforced concrete, or prestressed concrete).
- Windows and doors in the outer skin are to be built in compliance with RC2 or better.

Implementation of the mandatory requirements

This section also concretizes Section 8.1.1. This deals in more detail with the requirements for the outer skin of your building. The outer skin must be so stable that it cannot be penetrated by burglars using "commercially available tools". Commercially available tools are likely to include hammers or bolt cutters, for example. This also includes electric hammers or chisels.

Specialized tools, such as those used by the fire service or the German *Technisches Hilfswerk* (THW), are outside the scope of commercially available tools. Such tools have recently been increasingly stolen by gangs of thieves from fire brigades and used in sometimes spectacular break-ins. Nevertheless, such tools need not be included here. Attempted break-ins using vehicles (e. g. heavy construction vehicles or armored vehicles) or the use of explosives can also be disregarded here, as these are not commercially available tools either.

Implementation of the should requirements

The requirement for the outer skin is specified here. The outer skin should be solid, in the form of concrete or masonry.

Difficulties can arise for companies. It is conceivable, for example, that a company shares a hall with other companies and the separation here is only ensured by lightweight walls or other wooden walls. As the neighboring companies are outside the scope of the ISMS in accordance with TISAX, such partition walls are to be regarded as an outer skin. The "should" requirement would therefore not be fulfilled here. At the same time, it is not always possible or economically viable to retrofit a concrete wall for various reasons. As this is a "should" requirement, there is some room for maneuver here for an alternative solution that also allows other materials that offer a similarly high level of safety or load-bearing capacity as concrete or masonry. Arguments can be made here, for example, about the load-bearing capacity per square meter of the alternative material compared to a standard concrete wall or concrete ceiling.

Windows and doors must offer RC2 class protection. This also includes protection against being forced open.

8.1.4 To what extent is view and sight protection ensured in defined security areas?

Quote from ISA 6.0.3

It must be ensured that unauthorized viewing of vehicles, components or parts classified as requiring protection is prevented.

Must

- Unauthorized viewing of new developments needing high or very high protection is not possible.

Should

- Sight protection through relevant glass surfaces is ensured.
- View into defined security areas through open doors/gates/windows is prevented.

Additional requirements for vehicles classified as requiring protection

- The spatial situation is also suitable for protecting vehicles classified as requiring protection against unauthorized view.

Implementation of the mandatory requirements

This section also specifies Section 8.1.1. This deals in more detail with the requirements for privacy protection.

Access protection must always be guaranteed. Unauthorized persons must not have access at any time. This can be ensured by permanent or temporary measures, depending on the situation on site.

You should therefore include specifications for permanent and temporary visual protection in your security zone concept. The temporary measures must be closely linked to visitor management and project management. For example, it may be necessary to take measures for temporary privacy protection in good time before the arrival of certain visitor groups, e. g. by erecting privacy screens. This in turn is also linked to project management. Specifically, when and where certain prototypes are temporarily set up.

Implementation of the should requirements

This is about privacy protection through glass surfaces and through open doors or gates.

Permanent privacy protection through glass surfaces can easily be achieved by using mirrored glass or by attaching films. Roller blinds or venetian blinds can also be suitable, but there is a risk that these could be opened by careless employees or service providers.

Protection from view through open doors, windows or gates can be achieved, for example, by using curtains or privacy screens behind them.

You describe both of these in your security zone concept.

You should also review the effectiveness of these measures yourself in your regular internal audits (see Section 1.5.1).

Implementation of the additional requirements "for vehicles classified as requiring protection": The requirement here is that prototype vehicles must also be protected from view. If you have implemented the measures described above, there is nothing further for you to do here.

8.1.5 To what extent is the protection against unauthorized entry regulated in the form of access control?

Quote from ISA 6.0.3

It must be ensured that all points of access to security areas where vehicles, components or parts classified as requiring protection are manufactured, processed, or stored are protected against unauthorized entry by adequate measures.

Must

- At least one of the following three requirements must be implemented:
  - Mechanical locks with documented key assignment
  - Electronic access systems with documented authorization assignment
  - Personal access control including documentation.

Additional requirements for vehicles classified as requiring protection

- The spatial situation is also suitable for protecting vehicles classified as requiring protection against unauthorized access.

Implementation of the mandatory requirements

This section also specifies Section 8.1.1. This deals in more detail with the requirements for access protection.

The standard offers three possible types of access protection, at least one of which must be implemented:

Use of mechanical locks: You use "classic" locks with a physical key to protect all premises in which prototypes are stored. The issuing of keys must be documented, although this is already prescribed and regulated in more detail in Section 4.1.1. When issuing keys, also ensure that a "least privilege principle" is applied. This means that only persons with an authorized interest in accessing rooms in which prototypes are stored may be given keys. If not already in place, locks must be installed in internal rooms as required so that only authorized employees within the company can access these rooms. The issuing of keys is documented – individually numbered keys are recommended for better traceability.

Electronic access systems with documented authorization allocation are also an option. These are e.g. chip cards or transponders. The same applies here as described above for mechanical locks.

Personal access control, including documentation, only makes sense if mechanical locks or electronic locking systems cannot be used for structural reasons or if plant security staff are in the immediate vicinity anyway.

Implementation of the additional requirements "for vehicles classified as requiring protection": Here, the standard explicitly requires that prototype vehicles are also protected against unauthorized access by the "mandatory requirements" of this section. If you park prototype vehicles in garages, under canopies or in the open air, you may need to take further measures.

You describe the implementation of the requirements of this section in your security zone concept.

8.1.6 To what extent are the premises to be secured monitored for intrusion?

Quote from ISA 6.0.3

It must be ensured that premises where vehicles, components or parts classified as requiring protection are manufactured, processed, or stored are monitored for intrusion. Timely alarm processing is ensured.

Must

- Intrusion monitoring of the premises to be secured is ensured:
  - An intrusion detection system exists which complies with DIN EN 50131 or conforms to VDS or similar and functions with alarm tracking to a

    certified security service or control unit (e.g., according to DIN 77200, VdS 3138)
  - Or 24/7 guarding by a certified security service
- Alarm plans are available.
- Timely alarm processing is ensured.

Implementation of the mandatory requirements

In addition to the measures described, the operation of intruder alarm systems is prescribed by the standard for those rooms in which prototypes are stored.

These must be DIN EN 50131 or VDS-compliant systems with an alarm function to a certified security service. Simple systems such as low-cost glass breakage detectors are not an option here.

The standard does not specify which standard a security service should be certified to. Certification in accordance with ISO 9001 or DIN 77200 is conceivable, so make sure that a suitable and valid certification is available before commissioning the security service. As a service provider, you evaluate the security service as part of your supplier evaluation, as described in Section 6.1.1.

If you have not already done so, expand your emergency plan (see Section 1.6.3) to include the scenario of an intrusion report and define a specific alarm plan. To do this, liaise with your contracted security service. In the alarm plan, you define, among other things, which persons within the company should be informed in the event of a burglar alarm, how (e.g. by email, text message) and at what frequency. Overall, prompt alarm tracking must be ensured, especially by the contracted security service.

You describe the implementation of the requirements of this section in your security zone concept.

8.1.7 To what extent is a documented visitor management in place?

Quote from ISA 6.0.3

Protection against unauthorized access to security areas where vehicles, components or parts classified as requiring protection are manufactured, processed, or stored, including traceable documentation.

Must

- Registration obligation for all visitors.
- Documented non-disclosure obligation prior to access.
- Publication of security and visitor regulations.
- Country-specific legal provisions regarding data protection are to be observed.

Implementation of the mandatory requirements

You ensure that all visits are documented. In itself, Section 8.1.7 only requires this for rooms or areas in which prototypes are stored. In practice, it is easiest for most companies to document every visit to their premises.

You therefore adapt your visitor management regulations (see "Should requirements" in Section 3.1.1) in your security zone concept accordingly. Every visitor is therefore obliged to register, and every visit is documented. In addition, have each visitor sign a confidentiality agreement, which also obliges the visitor to refrain from filming and photographing. You can create a standard form for this purpose, which is available at the visitor entrance. Keep the signed originals and provide visitors with a copy on request.

The standard also requires you to publicize visitor and security regulations. You can include these in your confidentiality agreement and/or post notices at visitor entrances and within your premises.

Visitor management may also make it necessary to prevent visitors from bringing in devices that can be used for filming and photography, or to tape up such devices or store them for the duration of the visit. In addition to the "classic" camera, such devices also include smartphones or wearables with a photo function. See also the guidelines on photography in Section 8.2.6.

You can also add the aspect of "signage" to your security zone concept in order to specify that signs indicating that photography is prohibited must also be posted in the appropriate places.

As visitors' personal data must be recorded when they register, you are obliged to delete this data after a certain period of time (depending on your regional jurisdiction). If the visitor data is stored electronically, expand your deletion concepts to include this data. If you record visitor data additionally or exclusively in paper form, regularly check whether it is necessary to destroy the lists. You can add a permanent task to your centralized list of measures for this purpose. Use a shredder of level P4 or higher for the destruction or commission a specialized company. If you have a data protection officer, he or her should be involved.

8.1.8 To what extent is on-site client segregation existent?

Quote from ISA 6.0.3

In order to ensure protection of the client-specific know-how at all times, a clear segregation of clients must be ensured. This particularly involves protection against unauthorized viewing and access to areas where vehicles, components or parts classified as requiring protection are processed or stored.

Must

- Spatial separation by staff-related or technical measures is in effect according to the following aspects:
  - Customers, and/or
  - Projects
  - Where segregation is not in effect, explicit approval by the customer is required

Additional requirements for vehicles classified as requiring protection

- The spatial situation is also suitable for implementing client segregation for vehicles classified as requiring protection.

Implementation of the mandatory requirements

This section deals with the spatial separation of clients at your company's locations. Clients refers to various parties, in particular your various customers. The aim is to prevent one client from gaining access to the prototypes of another client. Please note: This section does not deal with the separation of clients for different users in software environments.

To implement the requirements, first check how many different clients there are that could potentially gain insight into or access to prototypes. As clients, consider your customers as well as the employees and partners involved in the project.

You have already fulfilled some of the requirements by implementing the access controls (see Section 8.1.5). However, there are also cases in which access controls alone are not sufficient. Think of visitors who move around your premises. Even if they are constantly accompanied by your employees, without sufficient visual protection measures in place, they could possibly see prototypes of other companies. Another risk for client separation lies in shared project premises.

You therefore define the measures you consider necessary for client separation and then implement them, whether these are technical, structural or organizational measures for visitor management. If client separation is not possible or not desired by your company, you will need documented authorization from your customers.

Implementation of the additional requirements "for vehicles classified as requiring protection":

Here, the standard expressly requires that the "mandatory requirements" of this section also protect prototype vehicles from inadequate client separation. If you park prototype vehicles in garages, under canopies or in the open air, you may need to take further measures.

You describe the implementation of the requirements of this section in your security zone concept.

8.2 Organizational requirements

Quote from ISA 6.0.3

The requirements described in this section apply to all companies which manufacture or are provided for use vehicles, components or parts classified as requiring protection.

This section aims to define various organizational requirements for prototype protection. Prototype protection is to be further increased through contractual agreements and internal workflows.

8.2.1 To what extent are non-disclosure agreements/obligations existent according to the valid contractual law?

Quote from ISA 6.0.3

When transmitting information classified as requiring protection, it must be ensured that external organizations are obliged to meet the information security requirements and that the related necessary measures are implemented. The necessary legal basis for this obligation is provided by non-disclosure agreements. Hence, it must be ensured that information classified as requiring protection is transmitted only if such a non-disclosure agreement has been entered and is legally effective.

Must

- A non-disclosure agreement:
  - Between contractor and customer (company level)
  - With all employees and project members (personal obligation)
- Country-specific legal provisions regarding data protection are to be observed.

Implementation of the mandatory requirements

Firstly, you conclude non-disclosure agreements with your clients – usually the OEMs in this case – with regard to prototypes. As it is in the client's own interest to protect themselves, they will normally initiate the signing of such agreements.

If the client does not do this, you must make them aware of this. According to the standard, you may only handle prototypes for the client if there is a sufficient non-disclosure agreement at company level.

In addition, check whether all your employees are sufficiently committed to confidentiality. This should be the case if you have already implemented the requirements from Section 2.1.2.

As the personal data of employees is recorded when they are personally engaged, you are obliged to delete the data you have stored after a certain period of time. You should therefore add this data to your deletion concepts. If you have a data protection officer, they should be involved.

8.2.2 To what extent are requirements for commissioning subcontractors known and fulfilled?

Quote from ISA 6.0.3

When involving subcontractors, the minimum requirements for prototype protection must be met.

Must

- Approval by the original customer.
- Contractually valid non-disclosure agreement exists:
  - Between contractor and subcontractor (company level)
  - With all employees and project members of the subcontractor (personal obligation).
- Ensuring compliance with the security requirements of the actual customer (proof is obtained).
- Proof of the subcontractor's compliance with minimum requirements for prototype protection (e.g., certificate, attestation) is provided.

Implementation of the mandatory requirements

You check whether the subcontractors you commission are sufficiently bound to confidentiality with regard to prototypes. You have already defined the process for dealing with non-disclosure agreements for subcontractors (companies, freelancers, etc.) if you have implemented the requirements from Section 6.1.1. At this point, you should check whether sufficient non-disclosure agreements have actually been concluded with all subcontractors who have access to prototypes. You should also check whether these have been formulated with sufficient legal certainty with regard to prototypes or whether they need to be supplemented.

You shall also require the subcontractors concerned to place each of their freelance or salaried employees under a personal obligation of confidentiality about prototypes if they have access to them. You shall obtain written confirmation from each subcontractor concerned that it has personally bound all of its employees to secrecy with regard to prototypes.

8.2.3 To what extent do employees and project members evidently participate in training and awareness measures regarding the handling of prototypes?

Quote from ISA 6.0.3

In trainings/awareness seminars on the subject of prototype protection, employees must obtain the necessary knowledge and skills for a security-conscious handling of vehicles, components and parts classified as requiring protection.

Must

- Ensuring execution of trainings/awareness programs by the management.
- Training of employees and project members when joining the project regarding the handling of prototypes.
- Regular (at least annual) training of employees regarding the handling of prototypes.
- Ensuring knowledge among employees and project members regarding the respective protection needs and the resulting measures within the company.
- Mandatory participation of each employee and project member in the trainings and awareness measures.
- The completed measures are to be documented.
- The training concept for prototype protection is an integral part of the general training concept (see also control question 2.1.3 Information Security).

Implementation of the mandatory requirements

You expand your existing training concept (see Section 2.1.3) to include the following training content on prototype protection:

- Dealing with prototypes in general
- Protection needs of prototypes and resulting measures

The training sessions must take place at least once a year and are mandatory for all employees, not just those directly involved in prototype projects. You document the participation of all employees by name.

In addition, always train project participants at the start of the project if the project is related to prototypes. It is a good idea to define a standard procedure for project management. This should include training on prototype protection at the start of the project. You may have already defined a standard procedure for projects when implementing the requirements from Section 1.2.3, which you can now extend.

8.2.4 To what extent are security classifications of the project and the resulting security measures known?

Quote from ISA 6.0.3

It must be ensured that the security classification and requirements in relation to the project progress are known to and observed by each project member.

Must

- Ensuring that the security classification and requirements in relation to the project progress are made known to each project member.
- Consideration of step-by-step plans, measures for secrecy and camouflage, development policies.
- The requirements are considered as a requirement regarding the information security of the project (see Controls 1.2.3 and 7.1.1 Information Security).

Implementation of the mandatory requirements

As part of the project management of prototype projects (see Section 1.2.3 and Section 8.2.3), ensure the following:

- All project participants are continuously informed about security classifications and the security requirements depending on the progress of the project.
- All project participants are continuously informed about changes to stage plans, confidentiality and camouflage measures and development guidelines.

How you implement these measures is not specified in detail by the standard. It makes sense to send information by e-mail, which also serves as proof. You should also consider verbal briefings and have the currently valid requirements available in some kind of "project folder" for all project participants. This makes it easy to find the current requirements and refer to them at any time.

8.2.5 To what extent is a process defined for granting access to security areas?

Quote from ISA 6.0.3

A process is defined for the protection against unauthorized access to security areas where vehicles, components or parts classified as requiring protection are manufactured, processed, or stored.

Must

- Responsibilities for access authorization are clearly specified and documented.
- A process for new assignments, changes and revocations of access rights is in place.
- Code of conduct in case of the loss/theft of access control means.

Implementation of the mandatory requirements

This section deals with the definition of access authorizations and the issuing of access resources, such as keys or transponders.

If you have already dealt with the requirements of Section 3.1.1 and Section 8.1.5, then you have already made provisions for this in your security zone concept and, if applicable, other procedural instructions. It therefore remains for you to check the measures you have taken to ensure that they take sufficient account of all rooms and properties in which prototypes are stored.

Rules of behavior in the event of loss or theft of locking devices include the following:

- Invalidation of the means of access by withdrawing access authorizations for electronic means of access or, if necessary, replacement of the locking cylinders for physical keys (see Section 4.1.1, ideally you should describe your regulations on this in your security zone concept)
- Treatment of the loss or theft as an information security event (see Sections 1.6.1 and 1.6.2)

8.2.6 To what extent are regulations for image recording and handling of created image material existent?

Quote from ISA 6.0.3

Regulations for recording images of vehicles, components or parts classified as requiring protection must be defined in order to prevent unauthorized creation or transmission of such image material.

Must

- Approval procedures for image recording.
- Specification for classification/categorization of image material.
- Secure storage of image material.
- Secure deletion/disposal of image material no longer required.
- Secured transmission/shipping of image material to authorized recipients only.

Implementation of the mandatory requirements

Firstly, if you have not already done so, add assets from the "Photos of prototypes"-category to the inventory of assets. You can subdivide this into further subgroups such as photos of components, photos of prototype parts, photos of prototype vehicles, etc.

You then classify the protection requirements for these assets by expanding the information classification policy (see Section 1.3.2). This also includes regulations for the secure storage, transport and deletion of image material.

These regulations apply to both employees and visitors. It is therefore important to communicate possible photography bans, for example as part of employee training (see Section 2.1.3) or as part of visitor management (see Section 8.1.7).

Note the data carrier!

When dealing with image recordings, the storage media and transmission paths are particularly important. When pictures are taken with a camera, they are usually stored on SD cards. The SD cards should therefore be inventoried and also protected against unauthorized access. Secure storage of the SD card and secure "transport" within the company are particularly important. After all, the SD card is often removed from the camera in order to transfer the data to a computer first.

Great care should also be taken when using smartphones for prototype recordings! It is practical to transfer the recordings directly from the smartphone to a cloud storage. However, there is always a risk that other app operators will read the smartphone's image memory, especially when it comes to BYOD smartphones (bring your own device).

8.2.7 To what extent is a process for carrying along and using mobile video and photography devices in(to) defined security areas established?

Quote from ISA 6.0.3

A process is defined for carrying along and using mobile video and photography devices in(to) security areas where vehicles, components or parts classified as requiring protection are manufactured, processed, or stored. Unauthorized creation or transmission of image material must be prevented.

Must

- Specification for carrying along (e.g., sealed/unsealed, etc.).
- Specification for use (e.g., phone calls, photography, etc.).

Implementation of the mandatory requirements

In your visitor management regulations, described in the security zone concept, you define regulations for devices capable of taking photos and filming.

Here you regulate – both for your employees and for visitors – in which security zones such devices may be brought in and under which circumstances recordings or telephone calls may be made. Regulations could be as follows, for example: Visitors are generally not allowed to take photos or make film recordings. Before entering the yellow or red security zone, devices capable of taking photos or filming must be handed in. They will be handed back to the visitor when they leave.

You can also use signs or information boards to communicate and ensure the rules of use before entering the respective security zones.

Some companies stipulate that the lenses of such devices must be taped for the duration of the visit. This is another way of protecting yourself from unwanted images.

In addition to the classic camera, photo and film-capable devices also include smartphones and wearables (e. g. smartwatches), provided they can be used to take photos or film.

You describe the regulations made here in your security zone concept.

8.3 Handling vehicles, components and parts

This section aims to maintain the camouflage and secrecy of classified parts and vehicles during transport and storage.

8.3.1 To what extent are transports of vehicles, components or parts classified as requiring protection arranged according to the customer requirements?

Quote from ISA 6.0.3

While being transported, vehicles, components and parts classified as requiring protection must be protected against unauthorized viewing, unauthorized image recording and access.

Must

- A process for obtaining customer-specific requirements for the transport of vehicles, components and parts classified as requiring protection is described and implemented.
- The security requirements defined by the customer are known and observed.
- The logistics/transport companies explicitly approved by the customer are commissioned.
- A process for reporting any security-relevant events to the customer is described and implemented.

Section 8.3, Section 8.4 and Section 8.5 have a repetitive structure: Requirements for protection are to be determined, complied with and violations are to be communicated.

For the sake of clarity, we describe the implementation of all subsequent sections in Section 8.3.1 and highlight which aspects of the implementation proposal relate to which section.

In addition to existing security requirements, there may be project-specific requirements due to circumstances (e. g. shooting location) or specific requirements of the OEM.

It must be ensured that all these additional requirements are agreed with the OEM and are known to those involved in the project.

To do this, expand your existing project list (see Section 1.2.3) to include the necessary aspects for projects with prototypes that require protection.

If prototypes are handled very frequently, it is advisable to keep separate documentation for these projects.

The following aspects should be explicitly documented:

- Client requirements for the protection of prototypes (general)
- Client requirements for transport and storage
- Transport requirements (Section 8.3.1)
- Approved logistics and transport companies (Section 8.3.1)
- Requirements for parking and storing prototypes (Section 8.3.2)
- Client requirements for camouflage and test drives
- Requirements for the deployment and use of camouflage (Section 8.4.1)
- Approved test and proving grounds (Section 8.4.2)
- Rules of behavior during test operation (Section 8.4.2)
- Protective measures for test sites (Section 8.4.2)
- Requirements for operation on public roads (Section 8.4.3)
- Protective measures for test drives on public roads (Section 8.4.3)
- Behavioral rules for special situations such as breakdown, accident, theft (Section 8.4.3)
- Client requirements for events and shootings
- Requirements for handling prototypes at public events (Section 8.5.1)
- Link to the security concepts and rules of conduct for events and shootings approved or provided by the client (Section 8.5.1 and Section 8.5.2)

- Requirements for photo shoots (Section 8.5.2)
- Authorized locations for shootings (Section 8.5.2)
- Additional requirements of your own company based on individual project situation
- Including any company-specific procedures derived from the OEM's requirements to fulfil the requirements
- Reporting requirements and deadlines in the event of a breach of security requirements, including the client's contact details
- General notification in the event of a breach of the protective measures
- Notification of changes to the camouflage (Section 8.4.1)
- Notification of exceptional occurrences on test sites (Section 8.4.2)
- Reporting incidents on public transport (Section 8.4.3)

The person responsible for the project should be committed:

- Determine and document the client's requirements and any necessary additional security measures before the start of the project
- Use the list of aspects mentioned above and ideally have this documentation approved by the client.
- Coordinate changes to the handling of prototypes with the client, taking into account the documented measures (e. g. when changing the camouflage)
- Identify and document the reporting requirements and deadlines in the event of a breach of the client's security requirements and contact details
- Investigate security breaches immediately and communicate them to the client
- Obtain all customer requirements in writing where possible
- Where possible, changes must also be agreed in writing with the customer.
- Random compliance checks during the course of the project
- Communication of the requirements to all internal and external project participants before the start of the project

Ideally, you should document the obligations of the project manager in a "Handling of prototypes" document (in which recurring requirements, e. g. for all projects of a specific OEM, can also be recorded in principle).

The project participants must be aware of all the specifications for the work on the prototype. Therefore, all requirements should be communicated by the project manager to the project participants in good time. Make sure that all aspects documented in the project list are taken into account.

As suggested in Section 8.2.4, an overview of the applicable requirements, rules of conduct and reporting requirements ("project folder"), which is available to all project participants, is suitable for this purpose. Alternatively, an overview that you send to all project participants via email would also be conceivable.

Ideally, you should have all project members confirm compliance in writing (e. g. as a reply to the email). Also bear in mind that external service providers may be involved in the project and need to be aware of the requirements.

8.3.2 To what extent is it ensured that vehicles, components, and parts classified as requiring protection are parked/stored in accordance with customer requirements?

Quote from ISA 6.0.3

While being parked/stored, vehicles, components and parts classified as requiring protection must be protected against unauthorized viewing, unauthorized photography, and access.

Must

- The customer-specific requirements for parking/storage are verifiably known and observed.

Implement Section 8.3.1 including the chapter-specific sub-aspects.

8.4 Requirements for test vehicles

Quote from ISA 6.0.3

A process for obtaining customer-specific requirements for the handling of test vehicles classified as requiring protection is described and implemented. The requirements described in this chapter are not relevant to components and parts.

When using own properties, the controls described in Clauses 8.1, 8.2 and 8.3 must also be verified. When not using own properties, merely the requirements of Clauses 8.2 and 8.3 must be met.

This section aims to obtain and implement the OEM's requirements for handling classified vehicles.

8.4.1 To what extent are the predefined camouflage regulations implemented by the project members?

Quote from ISA 6.0.3

It must be ensured, that the camouflage regulations are known to each project member and observed in order to guarantee adequate view protection of trial vehicles.

Must

- The requirements for using the respective camouflage are known to the project members.
- Any changes to the camouflage are made upon documented agreement with the customer.
- A process for the immediate reporting of any damages to the camouflage is described and implemented.

Implement Section 8.3.1 including the chapter-specific sub-aspects.

8.4.2 To what extent are measures for protecting approved test and trial grounds observed/implemented?

Quote from ISA 6.0.3

In order to maintain an undisturbed and secured trial operation on test and trial grounds, the respective protective measures defined by the customer must be observed.

Must

- A process for obtaining customer-specific requirements for the use of trial vehicles classified as requiring protection on test and trial grounds is described and implemented.
- The following aspects must be known to users of test and trial grounds:
  - A current list of customer-approved test and trial grounds
  - Code of conduct for ensuring undisturbed trial operation
  - Customer-defined protective measures These are implemented

Implement Section 8.3.1 including the chapter-specific sub-aspects.

8.4.3 To what extent are protective measures for approved test and trial drives in public observed/implemented?

Quote from ISA 6.0.3

It must be ensured that the respective customer requirements for the operation of test vehicles classified as requiring protection on public roads are known and observed.

Must

- A process for obtaining customer-specific requirements for the operation of test vehicles classified as requiring protection on public roads is described and implemented.
- Protective measures defined by the customer are known and observed.
- The code of conduct in case of special incidents (e.g., breakdown, accident, theft...) is known and observed.

Implement Section 8.3.1 including the chapter-specific sub-aspects.

8.5 Requirements for events and shootings

Quote from ISA 6.0.3

Customer-specific security requirements for events and shootings involving vehicles, components or parts classified as requiring protection are known to each project member. This must be demonstrated by each company commissioned with the planning, preparation or execution of events or shootings.

When using own properties, the controls described in Clauses 8.1, 8.2 and 8.3 must also be verified. When not using own properties, merely the requirements of Clauses 8.2 and 8.3 must be met.

This section aims to comply with and implement requirements and security measures relating to events and shoots.

8.5.1 To what extent are security requirements for presentations and events involving vehicles, components or parts classified as requiring protection known?

Quote from ISA 6.0.3

It must be ensured that the respective customer-specific security requirements for presentations and events involving vehicles, components or parts classified as requiring protection are known.

Must

- A process for obtaining customer-specific requirements for presentations and events involving vehicles, components or parts classified as requiring protection is described and implemented.
- Established and customer-approved security concepts (organizationally, technically, staff-related).
- Code of conduct in case of special incidents.

Implement Section 8.3.1 including the chapter-specific sub-aspects.

8.5.2 To what extent are the protective measures for film and photo shootings involving vehicles, components or parts classified as requiring protection known?

Quote from ISA 6.0.3

It must be ensured that the respective customer-specific security requirements for film and photo shootings involving vehicles, components or parts classified as requiring protection are known.

Must

- A process for obtaining customer-specific requirements for film and photo shootings involving vehicles, components or parts classified as requiring protection is described and implemented.
- Proof of approval for the presumably used premises.
- Established and customer-approved security concepts (organizationally, technically, staff-related).
- Code of conduct in case of special incidents.

Implement Section 8.3.1 including the chapter-specific sub-aspects.

The Authors

Bennet Vogel has set himself the goal of making the introduction of TISAX® as easy as possible for companies.

After training as an industrial clerk, he studied economics and graduated with degrees in economics. He then switched to management consulting and advised clients throughout Europe on management systems and improving their processes at the interface between customers and IT.

He has been working as a freelance consultant, auditor and trainer for management systems in Berlin since 2019. With over 16 years of experience as a management consultant and entrepreneur, he advises companies in all sectors on the introduction of management systems.

Bennet Vogel is a trained lead auditor for ISO 27001 and ISO 9001 and works as such for various certification bodies. Further training, including in risk management and customer journey mapping, round off his profile.

Contact:

bev@isoberater.de

www.isoberater.de/english

www.linkedin.com/in/bennetvogel

www.xing.to/bennetvogel

Responsible for chapters: 1.1.1, 1.3.1, 1.3.2, 1.3.3, 1.5.1, 1.5.2, 1.6.1, 4.1.1, 4.1.2, 4.1.3, 4.2.1, 5.2.1, 5.2.2, 5.2.3, 5.2.4, 5.2.5, 5.2.6, 5.2.7, 6.1.1, 6.1.2, 8.1.1, 8.1.2, 8.1.3, 8.1.4, 8.1.5, 8.1.6, 8.1.7, 8.1.8, 8.2.1, 8.2.2, 8.2.3, 8.2.4, 8.2.5, 8.2.6, 8.2.7

Christopher Eller is the founder of *isms-connect.com*. With his company, he has set himself the goal of making information security and compliance accessible to small and medium-sized companies. With works such as this book, content and best practices are made available to a wide audience.

After training as an IT specialist, he was responsible for IT purchasing, the introduction and migration of IT systems at a medium-sized automotive supplier. He was later responsible for the company's security strategy and, as Information Security Officer and Data Protection Officer, managed the data protection integration with the US parent company following a company acquisition.

Since 2017, he has focused on combining the experience he has gained in IT, compliance and security and making it accessible to companies.

Christopher Eller is an IHK-certified IT economist, TÜV®-Süd-certified as an ISO® 27001 auditor, data protection officer and risk manager with more than 14 years of experience in IT, security and compliance in the automotive industry.

Contact:

christopher.eller@isms-connect.com

https://isms-connect.com

http://www.linkedin.com/in/christopher-eller-isms

Responsible for chapters: 1.2.1, 1.2.2, 1.2.3, 1.2.4, 1.3.4, 1.4.1, 1.6.2, 1.6.3, 2.1.1, 2.1.2, 2.1.3, 2.1.4, 3.1.1, 3.1.2, 3.1.3, 3.1.4, 5.1.1, 5.1.2, 5.2.8, 5.2.9, 5.3.1, 5.3.2, 5.3.3, 5.3.4, 7.1.1, 7.1.2, 8.3.1, 8.3.2, 8.4.1, 8.4.2, 8.4.3, 8.5.1, 8.5.2

Index

E

G

H

I

J

K

L

M

N

O

P

www.ingramcontent.com/pod-product-compliance
Lightning Source LLC
LaVergne TN
LVHW081928200926
848484LV00009B/2394